50 SERIOUSLY FUNNY BIBLE SKETCHES

Still For My 100% Perfect Girl

50 Seriously Funny Bible Sketches

DAVID BURT

Design for cover by CCD (www.ccdgroup.co.uk)

ISBN 978–1–84291–261–4

01 02 03 04 05 06 07 Printing/Year 10 09 08 07

KINGSWAY COMMUNICATIONS LTD
Lottbridge Drove, Eastbourne BN23 6NT, England.
Email: books@kingsway.co.uk

Printed in the USA

Contents

PART SIX: Contemporary

Performance and Copyright

Acknowledgements

Before we get into the sketches I want once again to set the record straight and tip my hat to everyone who has in any way helped put this collection together.

To everyone who over the years has helped keep my grey matter buzzing by sharing ideas, stories and mountains of enthusiasm, I give my grateful thanks. My thanks go also to the huge number of performers who have helped me put together the very first performances of many of the sketches in this collection: I couldn't have done it without you.

I'm not one to mention names, but special thanks go to Tom, Ella, Big James, Rich, Tina and of course to [insert your name here if you think I have, unforgivably, omitted you!].

Big thanks again to my family, friends and all at Cranleigh Baptist Church for so much love and support. I apologise for all the times my mind wanders in mid-conversation when something you say or do strikes me as amusing, only for it to reappear exaggerated out of all proportion in a sketch! (See if you can see yourself in any of these – believe me, most of you are in there somewhere!)

And, finally, to the many people up and down the country who invest their time and talent into performing drama at church services and events: without you, the past year of compiling this collection would have been somewhat futile! I pray that as you use this book, our God of creativity will inspire you and all who watch through his Spirit.

With love, Dave Burt

Preface

Welcome one and all to this collection of sketches and I hope that you enjoy putting them together and performing them. In 2000 I produced a collection called *50 Sketches About Jesus*, and in that book I warned there may be a volume two. Now seven years later, here it is!

In the Introduction to that book I wrote a short section with some hints and tips on using drama, running workshops and drama groups, getting laughs and writing your own sketches. For those of you who haven't got the first book, this section is repeated here. For those who have, many thanks and feel free to use the next pages to create a few paper aeroplanes!

Before You Begin

My aim in this part of the book is not to give rigid 'how-to' instructions, but rather to give some suggestions—more like an ideas factory—where the reader or listener will pick up some good tips but also dispense with anything not applicable to their situation.

The Use of Drama

Defending the use of drama in the communication of a Christian message may seem faintly odd in these pages, as it's fairly obvious that anyone purchasing this book is already sold on the idea. However, you may find this useful, as over the years the church has had a bit of a stormy relationship with the arts.

Nowadays, most of the church is open to the use of many creative art forms as part of its life and worship, but in the late sixties and seventies, it was a rather different story. As a result of the drug-induced music scene, a wave of dubious films being banned and the theatre becoming increasingly erotic, the church seemed to distance itself from any possible connection with the arts. Strumming a guitar was about as daring as it got, and the suggestion of using drama as part of worship would have been greeted in many quarters with gasps of outrage and calls for repentance!

My pastor became a Christian in the early seventies at about the same time as he was applying to various drama schools in London. He was offered places at a couple of very good schools, but the pressure from his new Christian friends eventually caused him to reject his offers. The terrifying end to this story is that the poor guy ultimately became a minister (only joking Pete!). This story perfectly illustrates the strained and uneasy relationship between the church and the arts at that time.

The central defence for using drama to communicate biblical truth is simply that the Bible is very dramatic. I am totally convinced that anyone who says that the Bible is boring has in all honesty never actually read it—unless the only bits they've come across are the genealogies. It's got the lot: love, war, peace, betrayal, miracles, violence, sex, murder and a message of hope—though not necessarily in that order. There's so much in it that when Hollywood attempts to make a film about it, they can only cover a few chapters at a time and the films last for about six-and-a-half hours. If you look at a lot of stories, particularly in the Old Testament, they make Quentin Tarantino's *Pulp Fiction* look like bedtime reading! The Bible *is* dramatic: our challenge is to present it in a way that will make people sit up and listen.

Advertisers plunge to whatever depths are necessary to package their products in a way that will make them irresistible to the consumer. 'Unless you buy our revitalising shampoo with added vitamins, minerals and essence of jojoba, your hair will be an unconditioned, greasy and dandruff-infested disaster area . . .' They, of course, are usually peddling lies, whereas we have an exciting and life-changing truth to share. How much more important, then, that we communicate it effectively.

If to do this we need to follow an example, we need look no further than Jesus himself. He recognised the value of engaging his listeners, and we see him doing this countless times in his method of speaking and, of course, supremely through his parables. By letting people listen to and watch drama (and maybe even take part), we involve more of their senses, so the message goes in at different levels. It is not simply heard, but also understood.

Who's it for and why?

We've established that drama is a good way of communicating the gospel, but we shouldn't just perform for the sake of it. We need to know *why* we are performing a particular piece. Always decide your objective before staging any piece of drama, as this will dictate which sketch you select. Is it to bring a biblical story to life, to illustrate a particular kind of behaviour and its consequences, or to challenge the audience's response to the gospel? There can be dozens of reasons like these to use drama, but we should be able to sum up in a sentence what our objective is in using it.

We must also consider who our audience will be. This may seem obvious, but many times groups put together a piece, often brilliantly, but it is totally inappropriate to the audience or setting. Always check the age and knowledge of Scripture of who you will be performing to before selecting which piece to do. The setting is also important; for instance, one piece may be perfect for a raucous youth event but not for a communion service! It's all common sense really, but absolutely vital that you get this right if you want to achieve maximum impact.

Words of warning

I don't wish to appear a gloom-monger, but as well as establishing who you're performing to and why, I have one little word of warning. However good a piece of writing may be, there is no such thing as an actor- or director-proof sketch. In other words, even with a complete script in front of you, there is still a lot of work to do. I'm sure we've all sat through some dire productions of Shakespeare plays, and we can hardly blame the bard himself for these disasters. A collection of sketches such as these here can only be a resource book; the success of the piece rests essentially with the group who put it together.

Be encouraged, though! God has made us creative beings, and I've seen some fantastic pieces of drama put together by groups with no professional training, just a love and an interest in using drama to serve God. Do your homework, be enthusiastic and go for it!

And finally . . .

Unless you are performing a full-length play (none included here, I'm afraid), your dramatic offering will more than likely form part of a larger presentation—whether that is a church service, youth group discussion, outreach evening or whatever. A sketch will have maximum effect if *everyone* involved in that wider programme knows its content and objective. There is no point 'doing drama because trendy churches do it'—that's a sure-fire way to get it dropped from your church's agenda because people won't see the point of it. A dramatic piece needs to contribute to the overall message, to be built upon and referred to, but not over-explained or done to death!

Something for the Kids

When I had the privilege of running seminars and workshops at the Kingsway Children's Ministry Conferences on using drama with children, the response was encouraging, so it is worth noting some of the key points here.

With children, the main reason to use drama is often not to perform, but to inform as they learn by actually doing. If you decide to use drama in a session with your children, it's always good to plan the whole session ahead of time. Here are some suggestions for a typical evening:

Warm-up

Begin by doing a mini-physical workout with them—something which is fun, but not too strenuous. As well as warming them up physically, do some facial workouts, e.g. opening the face as wide as possible, then scrunching it up as tight as possible, pretend to chew large and sticky toffees, and do horse-blows to limber up the lips. (The children will absolutely love all this!) Finally, a basic vocal warm-up is advisable; repeating some famous tongue-twisters is a good way to do this.

Games

After a warm-up, it's good fun to play a game or two. No particular style is necessary—you can use any good games that you know which involve a mixture of energetic dashing around and basic concentration.

Mini-drama exercises

Now you can move on to some exercises more directly related to drama skills.

Machines

Split the children into two groups and give them a few minutes to act out a machine of their own choosing, including its features, movements and noises. A little tip when using this exercise is to ban them from using a television; in my experience, about 60 per cent of children choose this and it can get a bit boring!

Character walks

Get the children to move their bodies on the spot, bending knees, leaning over and backwards, etc. When the leader shouts 'Freeze', they must hold their final position for ten seconds, then start to walk holding that pose. From this, they start to develop a character. As they walk around in silence, let them think about the character's name, age, job, hobbies, where they are going, etc. If you have time, spotlight a few of them and get the rest of the group to ask them questions while they stay in character. If this sounds a bit advanced for your children, be assured that, regardless of age, kids are absolutely brilliant at it!

Emotional freeze frames

Split the children into groups again, and give each of them an emotion, e.g. love, anger, grief, fear. In just a few minutes, they must come up with a freeze-frame illustrating that emotion. This can take the form of a realistic scene, or alternatively, a more surreal image suggesting that emotion. The groups then try and guess each other's emotions. Again, this exercise is very short and great fun, but more importantly it begins to use the children's creative abilities.

Main exercises

All the previous suggestions are a preamble to the central exercise, where you complete your objective to teach whichever story, gospel truth or moral you have selected. There are various methods of doing this.

Use the Bible text

Simply having a person narrate a story from Scripture, and working out actions and noises with the children, is a very basic but fun and effective way of letting the children learn by doing. You can also *narrate from a children's Bible*. These have excellent paraphrased versions of most of the main Bible stories, and can sometimes be easier to use as a narration than the Bible text itself.

Have a go at the creative process yourselves!

This may freak some people out, but start by simply writing your own paraphrases from either the Bible or a children's Bible. You can easily slip humour into the stories by making mention of current issues (England's football results, major news items, the latest gossip from the soap operas), popular celebrities or even people from your own church who are well known to the kids and audience if you are also performing—having made sure they are people with a good sense of humour and no tendencies towards paranoia!

Find suitable sketches

Sketch books are written as a resource, and I hope this one has many suitable sketches that you will be able to use in the course of time. There are lots of other books available with sketches suitable for children and, although scripted pieces may be a bit harder to put together, the end results are worth it.

Improvisations

If there's one word related to drama that scares people off, it's improvisation. Immediately images of *Whose Line Is It Anyway?* leap to mind, and people react by running a mile. Children however, with their natural lack of inhibition, love it! Decide on the story you want to work on, and get groups to improvise various scenes based on it. One of my favourites is to use verses from Proverbs: Proverbs 11:13, for example, speaks about gossiping, and you can get a group to improvise around this passage set in a doctor's surgery, at a bus stop or even in church!

Whichever style of drama you choose to use with children, always end your session with a question time to check what they have learnt, and to see if your objective has been achieved. If you've worked on a drama based on the story of Noah, ask the child playing Noah how they felt when the neighbours made fun of his strange hobby. Hopefully, they will not just have had fun doing the drama, but have inwardly digested the various lessons through the stories too.

Drama Groups

Many churches don't have drama groups, either because they are too small or because not enough people have the desire or talent to join one. I believe that the most successful drama groups are built on quality and not quantity of members, and with this in mind, may I draw your attention to Jesus' famous words: 'Where two or three come together in my name, there am I with them' (Matthew 18:20). Now I know this is slightly out of context, but the same principle applies! Obviously not everyone has a gift in the area of drama, but if there are just two or three people in your church with interest and talent, you have enough people to start a drama group. Over a third of the sketches in this book are two-handers. So, be encouraged. Get together, ask your leaders for support in what you want to do and then just go for it! Once you get up and running, other people may want to join in, but if not, don't panic. Just carry on in your small group and work on being a real blessing to everyone else using your God-given abilities.

However, I believe it is a fallacy that anyone, regardless of ability, should be allowed to join a drama group and perform in church. This may seem harsh and rather discouraging, but actually it is perfectly reasonable. I would absolutely love to be in the band at church, looking cool and trendy strumming a guitar, tickling the ivories or, best of all, whacking the drums. But in the musical department, I'm totally inept, and the worship leader would—in a lovely Christian way, of course—refuse my request to join the band. Why then do people think that anybody, regardless of ability, can join a drama group? Don't misunderstand me: I strongly believe drama is for everyone, and people with talent can run workshops and help those who purely enjoy it. But if you are running a *drama group*, don't feel obliged to let everyone join and be in your productions, purely because they fancy themselves as the new Pacino.

Two of the major problems in the church today are first, people with wonderful gifts who are either too scared to use them or haven't yet discovered them, and second, people who think they have a particular gift which they quite clearly haven't! That may sound somewhat harsh, but the crucial truth to grasp is that every single person *does have gifts*; we need to make sure that we all discover them and then use them for God's glory in the areas we have been given them.

How to Get Laughs

If someone could concoct a formula to guarantee laughter, they would become a millionaire overnight. Unfortunately, it's not quite that easy. One person may find something hilarious, while another will look on with a vacant stare. Some performers have a special gift for creating laughter, having to do seemingly little to cause hysteria, while others have to work really hard to drum up a few sniggers. Tommy Cooper, who certainly had a natural ability to create laughter, only had to walk on stage and his audience would be in convulsions. For most, though, it's not like that. Put simply, getting laughs is no laughing matter!

So, if comedy is a natural ability bestowed on a few, how can other people gain those elusive laughs? Well, nothing of course can replace natural ability and lots of experience, but there are some areas where laughs can be found . . . or indeed lost!

Comic timing

We hear about it so often, and it is at the very centre of truly great comic performances, but what is it? Above all, comic timing is a skill you learn as you gain more experience in front of audiences. It is the sixth sense of delivering the line not too early, but not too late, for maximum impact. Never deliver a line while the audience are still laughing, as they will miss what you have said. But don't wait until all the laughter has stopped, leaving an awkward silence, as this will kill off the pace and momentum. In effect, you should deliver the line just at the moment when the laughter is dying down but hasn't actually finished.

It's difficult to explain any further without becoming too formulaic, but I encourage you to watch live performances or recordings of comedy, and watch for the timing and its power to control the laughter.

Milking the cow

When a performer knows they have a funny line, they have fallen into a potential minefield if they are tempted to 'milk the line'. Milking is basically giving far too much emphasis to a line, when in actual fact, saying the line naturally will always be the funniest. Performers who do this are quite simply selfish! They spend the minute leading up to the line preparing to forcibly thrust the witticism on the audience, and in the process kill what the ensemble cast has been collectively trying to achieve.

The best although rather generalised advice I can give, is to keep your performance deadpan. As soon as you start looking smug and thinking that you're incredibly funny, you're not! A good way to stop any potential 'milkers' in their tracks, is to have a discipline in rehearsal, whereby when anyone starts to milk a line, the rest of the cast mime the action of milking a cow. This will usually embarrass the guilty party into stopping, and it's also great fun!

Creating a character

Strong characterisations are a key ingredient for any good performance, particularly in comedy, and the funniest characters are the ones that are the most believable. If you are interested in drama, one of the best things you can do is to observe people's behaviour patterns. I find it fascinating to visit my local Asda supermarket, buy a cappuccino in the café, and then to watch the hundreds of people going by, taking in all their individual movements, speech and nuances. An hour of this can provide a cauldron of ideas for characters.

I have been criticised in my time for rather over-the-top caricature performances, and while in a full-length play they can be unsuitable, for short sketches such as the ones in this book, I believe there can be a place for them. With a caricature performance there are no subtleties. What you see is what you get, and in a five-minute sketch, where there is no time for character development, this can be beneficial.

However you play a character, though, it must have a degree of believability, and in rehearsal it is good to play around with characters, spotlighting each other and asking questions to help give them a bit more depth. From this, the actor can make any necessary tweaks. Again, researching the great comic performers for tips is wise, and for characterisation you would be hard pushed to better Peter Sellers.

What to use and where to put it!

Staging and props are often overlooked, but careful attention to how to stage a piece and a few well-chosen props can create laughter before a line is even spoken. I'm not talking about elaborate set design, revolving stages and numerous costume changes, but simply a few basic touches. For instance, in a sketch with fishermen or thieves, put some thought into costumes: use wellie boots, huge jackets and funny hats or stripey tops, swagbags and balaclavas. A few props appropriate to the sketch are worthwhile, and they can also be quite funny—just imagine Pontius Pilate sitting at his desk playing with a child's wind-up toy!

The staging of a piece can also be crucial to its impact. Carefully consider where the audience will be, and place any props and furniture in the best position. This is especially important in a sketch which involves the cast sitting down to deliver lines.

Good script and direction

When an actor collects an award for best performance, how often does he or she pay tribute to the writer and director? Admittedly, this can be false modesty, as the actor has obviously had an influential part to play, but I believe that good comedy is very much a team effort—a mixture of performance, script and direction.

Personal taste naturally dictates what will make any individual laugh but, when looking for a comedy script, use one the group collectively finds funny. It's very important that you perform a piece that you all believe in. If the cast are quite simply bored or disillusioned with the piece they are performing, it makes for very stale viewing.

Good direction is also a key element in comedy. The director should preferably be someone who is not actually performing, but who has a good eye for what works on stage. They have a much better overall view of the piece by standing on the outside, and should be able to pick up on any humour which is simply not working. They should also direct when the pace of a piece needs to pick up.

The laughter of recognition

A very popular ingredient of successful comedy is to create laughter by recognition, commonly known as observational humour. This style is very much associated with stand-up comedy, but can also be employed in sketches. It requires the performer to devise a situation which the audience can immediately identify with. This can be an habitual human foible, a common and frustrating bureaucratic circumstance or just something that generally tends to happen to us all in life.

For instance, in a supermarket, whichever queue you choose, the next one seems to move faster and the person in front of you is always paying by cheque! Human beings also have a strange tendency to think that if you pick your nose in the privacy of your car while in a traffic queue, no one else in the world can see you! And on the subject of noses, why do we get to a certain age, then suddenly sprout nasal hair?

These may seem like silly examples, but they provide fertile ground for dramatic comedy. Think about funny things that happen to you in life, and the chances are they happen to lots of other people too.

In Your Own Write?

I would like to give any budding writers the encouragement to pick up their pens and have a go at scripting some sketches themselves. Unfortunately, a talent for good writing is something that some people possess and some don't, but you won't know until you put pen to paper and have a try.

Be warned that it can be a very slow process. Sometimes the ideas are free-flowing and you can't write fast enough, but at other times, it can be a real slog and you have to be very disciplined. Also, don't expect to get it right first time: my notebook is covered in huge crossings-out and scribbles.

Getting your ideas needn't be a hard task, it can actually be great fun. Go and see as many plays as you can, read lots of good books and keep your eyes open for current issues in the newspapers. I'm not proposing that you plagiarise someone else's work, but taking in as many creative forms as possible will give you ideas for suitable content and styles that will work when employed on the stage.

Always think of your 'target-audience' when writing: are you aiming at 'clued-up' Christians, or fringe people, or seekers, or the totally unchurched? Make sure you use language and situations which will be familiar and accessible.

You will also need to be willing to take some criticism from other people. I have been fortunate to have a group who have 'guinea-pigged' some of the sketches in this book, and they give me encouragement for things that really work, but also tell me (quite bluntly!) if something is a non-starter. I admit this can be tough when you've put hours of graft into something, but we need to realise that there are times when a situation that seems stupendously funny as you write at your desk can be a lame duck when actually put onto the stage. Find someone whose opinion you value, who will be constructive in their criticism, and make a vow not to get too over-defensive when at times they disagree with you.

Christmas

The Tone-Deaf Angel

'I don't mean to bear bad news, but you can't sing'

INTRODUCTION

With the onset of numerous talent and reality shows, I wonder what would have happened if that had been the norm when putting together the angelic throng! And just imagine if one of the angels had to go through the humiliation so often seen on our television screens of not realising they were completely tone-deaf. This piece works best if the humour of the first part is contrasted by the moving impact of the 'Do not be afraid' speech towards the end.

Characters: ONE; TWO; THREE; MASTER.

'Hark the Herald Angels Sing' is playing. ONE and TWO are sitting in a waiting area. THREE enters.

THREE:	Hello! Am I in the right place for the auditions?
ONE:	Yeah, this is it.
THREE:	(*Sits down*) Great. Are you nervous?
ONE:	Little bit, yeah. You?
THREE:	Me, nervous? No! Bit of an old hand at these things, to tell you the truth.
ONE:	It's my first one.
THREE:	Oh, don't worry, you'll do fine. Nerves are a good thing in small measure – gives you adrenalin, if you know what I mean.

ONE: I think so, yeah.

THREE: (*Turns to TWO*) What about you – your first time, is it?

TWO: No.

THREE: So you're not nervous, then?

TWO: No.

THREE: Not very chatty either, are you?

TWO: No.

THREE: But you think you have the X factor?

TWO: Oh, yes. True talent has a way of making itself known.

THREE: Yes, very good – that's the spirit! (*Turns back to ONE*) You can learn from this one. Doesn't look like a lead contender to be part of an angelic throng, though. (*MASTER enters*)

MASTER: Ah, welcome, welcome! Hope you've not been waiting too long.

THREE: No, no, not at all.

MASTER: As you know, we're making up a fairly standard angelic throng, but it's for a rather momentous occasion, so we need to be spot-on!

THREE: Ah, look no further!

TWO: (*Sneezes*)

THREE: Are you quite all right?

TWO: Yes, yes – I think I must have an allergic reaction to your wings.

THREE: Well, I'll try not to flap them in your vicinity!

TWO: Most grateful.

MASTER: Right, shall we make a start, then? Let's begin with a basic scale. (*Sings*) Do re me fa so la ti do. (*ONE, TWO and THREE all repeat, ONE and TWO in tune, THREE out of tune*)

MASTER: Oh dear! Shall we try that again? (*MASTER sings scale, followed by ANGELS, once more with ONE and TWO in tune and THREE out of tune*)

MASTER: I'm not sure you're all in tune.

THREE: Probably her – it's her first time.

ONE: Excuse me?

THREE: All I mean is, it's just beginner's nerves. I'm sure you have a very lovely voice.

MASTER: Well, we'll see. Can we try a 'Gloria', please? One at a time. I'll demonstrate. (*Sings long 'Gloria' from 'Hark the Herald Angels Sing'*) And first –

ONE: (*Sings 'Gloria'*)

MASTER: Very good. And you –

TWO: (*Sings 'Gloria'*)

MASTER: Lovely. And third –

THREE: (*Sings 'Gloria' out of tune*)

MASTER: My goodness!

THREE: Impressive, eh?

MASTER: Certainly original. Can I give you the scale one more time? (*Sings 'Gloria'*)

THREE: (*Once more sings terribly out of tune*)

MASTER: Yes. . . Have you ever sung before?

THREE: Of course, thousands of times.

TWO: In an angelic throng or a cats' choir?

THREE: Button it!

MASTER: When I say have you sung before, I mean in public.

THREE: Well, no – but every morning I sing in the shower, and you get a fantastic resonance off those porcelain tiles.

MASTER: Quite so. It's just – I don't want to bear bad news, but you can't sing.

TWO: Understatement of the year.

THREE: Can't sing?

MASTER: I'm afraid not.

THREE: So I've not got the X factor?

MASTER: No.

THREE: But it's my dream to be part of an angelic throng! I've been working on these wings for months.

MASTER: I'm terribly sorry.

THREE: Well, I want a second opinion.

TWO: Ooh, I'll give you one.

THREE: Not from you! (*To ONE*) You seem a kindly angel – what did you think?

ONE: Well, to be honest it was a touch off-key.

TWO: A touch?

THREE: I see. Well, that's that, then. Dream over. I knew I should have kept up the harp lessons. (*Starts to leave*) Well, I wish you all the best.

MASTER: Hang on a minute! I do have one part you may be interested in.

THREE: Really?

MASTER: It's quite a leading role, actually.

THREE: A leading role! Sounds perfect.

MASTER: Yes, but it's a speaking role.

THREE: A speaking role?

MASTER: Do you want to try it?

THREE: Go on, then, let's give it a go. (*MASTER hands him a sheet of paper and THREE reads meaningfully*) 'Do not be afraid. I bring you good news of great joy that will be for all the people. Today, in the town of David, a Saviour has been born to you. He is Christ the Lord.' (*Pause*) How was that?

MASTER: Very good. Very good indeed.

ONE: Well done.

TWO: Yeah, it was okay, I suppose.

MASTER: You've got the job. You'll be at the front of the throng. Deliver that message and the rest will chime in with 'Glory to God in the Highest'. Oh, it'll be astounding!

THREE: And can I sing along?

MASTER: Er, no!

THREE: How about very quietly?

MASTER: No. But I'll do you a deal – you can mime.

THREE: Mime? Good enough!

MASTER: Great. Now, I just need your details. What's your name?

THREE: It's Gabriel. The Angel Gabriel.

BIBLE REFERENCE
Luke 2:8–20

Ye Olde Tale of Ye Firste Christmas

'I think we'd prefer the truth, if it's not too much trouble'

INTRODUCTION

For this sketch Two becomes the complete bane of One's life! The performer playing One should play his or her part in full *Jackanory* mode, while Two is sarcastic and irritating beyond words. I'm sure most church groups have got someone that fits that description!

Characters: ONE; TWO.

ONE is onstage, TWO is seated in the audience.

ONE: Are you all sitting comfortably? Well then, let's begin 'Ye olde tale of ye firste Christmas'. (*Lights change to spotlight*) Many, many years ago in a faraway place lived an attractive young couple by the name of Mary and Joseph. Upwardly mobile and happily married, they were filled with joy, as they were expecting their first child, due at any time.

TWO: (*From audience*) Well, that's a load of rubbish for a start.

ONE: (*Pause; then apologises to the audience for the interruption*) I'm sorry about that. As I was saying – upwardly mobile and happily married they were –

TWO: And off he goes again!

ONE: (*To audience*) I'm sorry. (*To TWO*) What is your problem?

TWO: Well, to be frank, *you* are! 'Upwardly mobile and happily married' –what a pile of pants!

ONE: So you don't like my story?

TWO: It's not that – it's just not true, is it? Joseph and Mary were
      not married.

ONE: Ah, I see where you're going with this. But it's hardly the
      central point of the story, is it? I mean, talking about ille-
      gitimate pregnancies is not really appropriate in a festive
      celebration, especially when there are impressionable
      young children present.

TWO: Children or no children, I think we'd prefer the truth, if
      it's not too much trouble.

ONE: Okay then, if that's your attitude. (*Starts again*) Many,
      many years ago in a faraway place lived an attractive
      young couple called Mary and Joseph. Downwardly
      mobile and recently engaged, Mary was unfortunately up
      the duff and Joseph was thinking about getting a quickie
      divorce.

TWO: Much better!

ONE: Thank you very much. May I continue now?

TWO: Please, be my guest.

ONE: So kind. Even under these terribly trying circumstances
      Joseph and Mary loved each other deeply. But about that
      time Caesar called for a census of all the people in his
      lands. Because Mary was with child, they were given a
      special dispensation to register in the region of Nazareth
      where they lived.

TWO: You're joking!

ONE: What now, for Pete's sake?

TWO: They had to register in Bethlehem, you hopeless dork.

ONE: Look, I'm getting fed up with your interruptions and
      brash rudeness.

TWO: Well then, get your facts straight and I won't have to!

ONE: What difference does it make if they register in Nazareth
      or Bethlehem?

TWO: Er, none, except one is true and one is made up.

ONE: Look, I'm a professional storyteller, and in my profes-
       sional opinion the whole 'travelling on a donkey to Beth-
       lehem' thing slows down the narrative.

TWO: Tough! It's not your job to edit.

ONE: Right! (*Starts again*) About this time Caesar called for a
       census of all the people in his lands. Joseph and Mary had
       to register in Bethlehem, and because Mary in her weak-
       ened state found travel tiresome, Joseph popped down
       the local pet shop and bought a mangy old donkey to
       carry his heavily pregnant wife.

TWO: Fiancée!

ONE: *Fiancée!*

TWO: See – easy, isn't it? Carry on, Macduff.

ONE: (*Starts again*) Bethlehem was a quiet and sleepy village,
       famous for absolutely nothing. Mary and Joseph arrived
       in the dead of night seeking accommodation to rest after
       their exerting travels. Fortunately, Bethlehem had a num-
       ber of inns, hostels and hotels, but, as Joseph wandered
       from one to the next, they all displayed 'no vacancy'
       signs. A top-of-the-range Radisson hotel was their last
       hope, and on enquiring about a possible vacancy Joseph
       was delighted to hear about a recent cancellation. The
       ensuite room offered was fit for a king. Super king-sized
       bed, minibar, trouser press, sandal rack and a complimen-
       tary shower cap were just some of –

TWO: I can't stand this any longer!

ONE: Well, why am I not surprised?

TWO: I mean, come on – a sandal rack!

ONE: I think that sounds very sensible.

TWO: And a complimentary shower cap!

ONE: It's called dramatic licence.

TWO: No, it's called gibberish!

ONE: Well, perhaps you can do better.

TWO: Yes, I think I probably could.

ONE: Come on then, clever clogs – give it a go.

TWO: Right. (*TWO moves from audience to stage*) On arrival in Bethlehem Mary and Joseph discovered all the rooms were occupied, but a kindly innkeeper took pity and gave them use of his stable area. Thus Mary gave birth to Jesus surrounded by cows, donkeys, bales of straw, infestations of flies and oodles of animal pooh.

ONE: Oh, really – I must protest!

TWO: The truth hurts, doesn't it?

ONE: You literalists drive me bonkers! You have to spoil the beautiful innocence of the story by making it all filthy dirty.

TWO: But much more accurate, wouldn't you say?

ONE: No! And if you don't mind, this is my story and I object to the 'p' word.

TWO: What 'p' word?

ONE: What do you think? Pooh!

TWO: Oh! Well, I've no objections to a few minor changes.

ONE: Thank you. Shift over. (*Gets back on stage and resumes story*) On arrival in Bethlehem, Mary and Joseph discovered all the rooms were occupied, but a kindly innkeeper took pity and gave them the use of his surprisingly well-equipped stable. Thus Jesus was born in relative comfort, albeit within the presence of some rather earthy and natural aromas. (*To TWO*) Happy?

TWO: I suppose so. It's the best we're going to get. What is the point of this story, anyway?

ONE: How ignorant! Everyone knows!

TWO: Go on, then.

ONE: Well, it reminds us that Christmas is about his story – you know, Jesus and stuff. And not about presents and tinsel and turkey!

TWO: How boring! We all know that cliché, 'put the Christ in Christmas', but what's it all about, really?

ONE: I don't know. I'm just the storyteller. But all this lot know
        what it's about, don't you?
        Don't you?

BIBLE REFERENCE
Matthew chapters 1–2

Carrots with Garlic Dip

'Do you know how far it is from Nazareth to Bethlehem? Well, I'll tell you – it's a flipping long way!'

INTRODUCTION

Here is the account of the journey from Nazareth to Bethlehem from the point of view of the poor donkey that carried Mary. It is a monologue that is best learnt, but could easily be performed as a dramatised reading.

Character: DONKEY.

DONKEY: They've got me in this retirement home now. Mount Lodge, it's called. Not very original, is it? Mind you, I shouldn't complain – it's done up lovely. Beautiful stables – the decoration is impeccable. And three meals a day: carrot for breakfast, carrot for lunch and carrot for tea. Not a great variety, I admit, but it's always fresh, I'll give them that. And I don't mean to gossip, but some of the other donkeys in here – well, to be honest, they've seen better days. One's got an eye missing, there's a couple with water on the knee, there's one with a wonky ear and another one who has got the worst case of halitosis I have ever encountered. It's enough to make you bray!

       Still, all things considered, I suppose I've seen better days myself. My back's never been right, not since my

headline-grabbing journey carrying you-know-who.
And here at Mount Lodge I get respect for that. I'm
the official top donkey, so to speak. No, when the new
ones arrive it's only a matter of hours before I'm being
pointed out by the others – 'Look, that one over
there! That's the one that carried her all the way from
Nazareth to Bethlehem.'

As if I needed reminding, with a permanent curve
in my spine!

Seems amazing, though, that it all happened the
best part of eight years ago. I'd been up for sale in this
shop called 'Sylvia's Pet Emporium' for I don't know
how long. And in all that time no one had given me
even a sideways glance. Every time a potential customer was in the shop I tried my hardest to look cud-
dly and cute, but to be honest it's a bit tricky when
you've got a set of teeth like Janet Street-Porter! Then
one day, out of the blue, in comes this chap, looking
a bit harassed. He comes straight up to me, gives me a
quick once-over, and then declares I'm perfect –
exactly what he's looking for. So he pays up and off I
trot, new horizons sprawling before me. Or so I
thought.

When we got home it was obvious fairly quickly
we were about to take a trip. There were bags packed
all over the place and no obvious spot for me to take
a much-deserved rest. And just when I thought things
couldn't get any worse, *she* appeared – my new mis-
tress. To describe her as 'pregnant' would be under-
stating it – she looked fit to burst! And it soon became
apparent that not only was I expected to carry all their
worldly possessions, but her as well, bump included!
In the light of how things turned out, I should be
grateful for the privilege, but at the time I was seriously

miffed! So would you have been. Do you know how far it is from Nazareth to Bethlehem? Well, I'll tell you – it's a flipping long way! Especially with that lot on your back. And the condition of the roads is terrible. I blame the Romans. None of your nice smooth tarmac – it was all bumpy and dusty. I was stumbling around all over the place, thinking my poor ankles will never be the same again. Every time I even slightly dipped my head I got an eyeful of grit and dust! Oh, it was the most miserable time of my life.

Anyway, after travelling for goodness knows how long, we arrived in Bethlehem. The place was heaving with visitors, and of course his nibs, the brain of Nazareth, hadn't booked us a room! I ask you! Even I know you have to advance-book accommodation, and I'm a donkey! Eventually some generous chap offers us his stable. Not particularly suitable for a pregnant woman, but for a shattered donkey it was perfect. As soon as we got in there I went to the corner and crashed out. Then I slept. And I slept like I've never slept before or since.

While I was sleeping, some amazing things happened, apparently. A huge star appeared over the stable, indicating the birth of a king. The child was born, and there were visitors from far and wide bringing greetings and gifts. Some visitors even arrived on camels. I was very happy to have missed them – camels smell even worse than halitosis-breath over there!

When I finally awoke, I thought we might at least be spending a few days in Bethlehem, just to see some sights, but no such luck. The first thing I noticed was that all the bags were packed again, and there was even more stuff this time, what with all the baby gifts. The couple were clucking around, getting ready for the trip. I've no idea what all the rush was, but the destination, I overheard, was to be Egypt.

Imagine it! Nazareth to Egypt – my poor ankles! And it was an eventful trip, full of excitement and intrigue. But you'll have to wait and hear that story another day. I'm off for my supper, and it's my favourite today – carrot with a garlic dip. Lovely!

BIBLE REFERENCE
Matthew 2:13–15

The Nutshell Nativity

'Many, many years ago, in a place far, far away. . .'

INTRODUCTION

This ensemble piece is great fun to perform and allows your group to be original and creative in their delivery. I've never done it the same way twice, and although I have included some rough stage and action directions, the piece will be best if you come up with some of your own. The piece is narrated, but if you have a small group the words and music can be recorded in advance to save using one of the cast to narrate on the night. Make sense? Read on, and all will become clear!

Characters: NARRATOR; ENSEMBLE (of around four people).
Big, gala-style music to open the sketch. ENSEMBLE makes grand entrance.
NARRATOR: Ladies and gentlemen, take your seats as we proudly present the Nutshell Nativity!

(*More fanfare music*)

Many, many years ago, in a place far, far away. . .

(*ENSEMBLE mimes and hums creepy 'Twilight Zone' music*)

. . .there lived a beautiful, fair and innocent young couple – Mary. . .

(*MARY steps forward and says 'Hello'*)

. . .a master seamstress who enjoyed weaving taffeta tablecloths, and Joseph. . .

(*JOSEPH steps forward and says 'Hello'*)

. . .a rugged carpenter who enjoyed randomly banging nails into blocks of wood.

They had recently received an angelic visitation informing them that Mary was pregnant with a baby who was to become the Saviour of the World. This news they had received with an understandable degree of. . .

(*All ENSEMBLE members drop jaws and gasp, looking utterly shocked*)

. . .shock!

Shortly after this they had to travel to Bethlehem for a census.

Occupation? (*One person answers 'Chariot mechanic'*) Number of rooms in your property? (*One person answers 'Three'*) Number of occupants in house? (*One person answers 'Sixty-four'*) And available toilet facilities? (*One person answers 'A bucket in the garden'*) Joseph found a donkey for the journey. . .

(*One actor becomes the DONKEY and brays*)

. . .and saddled up Mary for the journey of her life.

(*MARY gets on the DONKEY and squeals. ENSEMBLE sings 'Little Donkey'. At one point on the dusty road one of the ENSEMBLE blows flour in the DONKEY's face.*)

It was a long journey over high hills. . .

(*DONKEY lurches up*)

> . . .down deep vales. . .

(*DONKEY dips down sharply*)

> . . .and when they arrived, Mary was very tired. . .

(*MARY does over-the-top 'tired' pose*)

> . . .and the donkey was completely exhausted.

(*DONKEY collapses*)

> The only space available for them to stay in all of Bethlehem was a smelly stable.

(*ENSEMBLE responds to smell*)

> And neither was the stable particularly clean.

(*ENSEMBLE responds, 'Ugh, filthy!'*)

> But as a makeshift maternity ward it served its purpose.
> They sent out for towels. . .

(*ENSEMBLE shouts 'Towels!'*)

> . . .hot water. . .

(*ENSEMBLE shouts 'Hot water!' One gets burnt – 'Aagghh!'*)

> . . .and Prozac to calm Joseph's nerves.

(*JOSEPH slumps*)

> The birth was, from a male perspective, pain-free.

(*MARY reacts: 'Huh!'*)

> Joseph comforted his wife with those immortal words. . .

(*JOSEPH says, 'Come on, dear, just push'*)

Mary responded by gripping his hand like a vice. . .

(*JOSEPH screams*)

. . .and in a strange voice she said. . .

(*MARY says, 'When this is over I'm going to brain you!'*)

. . .but when they saw the beautiful baby, their hearts melted.

The parents ahh-ed. . . (*ENSEMBLE goes 'Ahh'*)

The sheep baa-ed. . . (*ENSEMBLE goes 'Baa'*)

The cattle lowed. . . (*ENSEMBLE, confused, goes 'Uhh. . .?'*)

Oh, all right – moo-ed. . . (*ENSEMBLE, relieved, goes 'Moo'*)

News travelled fast, and it wasn't long before the special baby had attracted some important visitors. A group of wise men came from the East, riding on camels.

(*ENSEMBLE enacts this*)

All sporting long grey beards. . .

(*ENSEMBLE strokes imaginary beards*)

. . .and bearing gifts.

(*ENSEMBLE takes turns stepping forward and offering 'Gold', 'Frankincense', 'Myrrh' and 'Spiderman on DVD'*)

The wise men did peer into the manger, and with looks of joy they exclaimed. . .

(*ENSEMBLE 'Oo's a lovely ickle boy, den?'*)

A while later a group of shepherds came in from the fields sporting down-to-earth ruffian looks and bearing more gifts.

(*ENSEMBLE takes turns stepping forward and offering gifts. First three all say 'Sheep', and the fourth guiltily also says, 'Sheep. . . Well, I couldn't think of anything else.'*)

'How original,' thought Mary and Joseph. Then the shepherds peered into the manger and with looks of joy exclaimed. . .

(*ENSEMBLE, with rough voices, 'Oo's a lovely ickle boy, den?'*)

At that point the party really kicked off. There was laughter. . .

(*ENSEMBLE laughs*)

. . .singing of carols. . .

(*ENSEMBLE sings*)

. . .and other festive songs. . .

(*ENSEMBLE sings an annoying Christmas song*)

But the party was suddenly stopped. . .

(*ENSEMBLE freezes*)

. . .with news that the evil King Herod. . .

(*Evil music and poses*)

. . .had hatched a plan to try to kill the new-born babe. Escape to Egypt was the first plan.

(*ENSEMBLE gets into donkey-on-road pose*)

But that, as they say, is a story for another time.

(*Play 'Little Donkey' to close*)

BIBLE REFERENCE

Matthew chapters 1–2

Pair of Turkeys

'A sower went out to sow. . .'

INTRODUCTION

Here's a really silly one! Two turkeys talking about morals, the Middle East and Christmas – need I say more? Have fun with the costumes on these: perhaps some silly swimming cap on the head and a Marigold glove hanging under the chin!

Characters: ONE; TWO; FARMER (walk-on).

ONE is onstage reading a newspaper. TWO enters, clucking intermittently.

ONE: What are you doing?
TWO: Clucking.
ONE: Do what?
TWO: Clucking!
ONE: Why on earth are you clucking?
TWO: Well, it's just what I do.
ONE: Can't you speak English?
TWO: I can, but being a turkey I prefer to cluck. It seems more – natural.
ONE: Well, it sounds absolutely ridiculous.
TWO: Have you ever tried it?
ONE: No, I have not!
TWO: Well, don't knock it then.
(TWO continues clucking. ONE turns away to try to hide a failed attempt to cluck.

TWO notices him and tries to encourage him)

TWO: That's it – go on!

ONE: No. It's so demeaning.

TWO: Don't give up now!

ONE: I can't do it with you gawping at me.

TWO: That's your problem – no stick-ability.

ONE: Okay, you may have me on that, but at least I don't look a complete state like you.

TWO: What do you mean?

ONE: Look! What's that thing hanging off your face?

TWO: This?

ONE: Yes, that!

TWO: It's my caruncle.

ONE: Caruncle? Looks like a Marigold glove to me.

TWO: Well, it's not – it's a caruncle.

ONE: No, I'll tell you what it is – disgusting and ugly.

TWO: Have you, er, looked in the mirror recently?

ONE: No. I don't possess one.

TWO: Check yourself out in my compact.

ONE: (*Shocked*) Oh no! This day's becoming like a bad dream. Clucking noises, wobbly appendages. . .

TWO: Calm down! You just need to accept what you are, mate.

ONE: What?

TWO: You need to accept what you are.

ONE: (*Sarcastic*) That sounds like a moral, doesn't it, children?

TWO: It is.

ONE: You'd better say it again to make sure it goes in – this lot look a bit thick.

TWO: (*Slowly*) You need to accept what you are.

(*Pause. ONE continues to read. TWO fidgets and looks around*)

ONE: Terrible business in the Middle East, isn't it?

TWO: Mmm, some of the trouble is getting dangerously near to Turkey.

ONE: I've always had a soft spot for Turkey.

TWO: Probably the name, isn't it?

ONE: I wonder which came first?

TWO: What, the turkey or the egg?

ONE: No! The country or the bird.

TWO: Ooh, you are clever.

ONE: Comes from reading. Learning.

TWO: Hello – here comes the farmer.

(*Walk-on role – a FARMER throwing seed randomly*)

TWO: Look what a mess he's made! Most of the seed has fallen on the path.

ONE: Did you say on the path?

TWO: Yes, on the path.

ONE: Go on, once more, just to make sure they get it – they look a bit slow!

TWO: (*Dramatically*) The seed hath mostly fallen on the path.

ONE: Well, that's ridiculous. It won't be able to take root on the path.

TWO: The birds will peck it all up before you can say –

ONE: Wait a minute! I know this one – before they can say supercudgeafudgealistic– (*Spots TWO eating the seed*) Wait a minute, you greedy oik!

TWO: Don't get your caruncle in a twist! There's plenty here for both of us.

ONE: Yes, well, even so. (*Eats some*) This'll fatten us up nicely.

TWO: That's good, 'cos Christmas is coming in a couple of months.

ONE: Mmm. . . Why do turkeys fatten up for Christmas?

TWO: I don't know. It's just what we're meant to do.

ONE: Is that another one of your morals?

TWO: Yeah. (*They exit, following trail of seed*)

BIBLE REFERENCE
Mark 4:3–20

Extraordinary News

'Kids! Who'd have 'em?'

INTRODUCTION

This is a monologue from the viewpoint of Mary, mother of Jesus. Like most monologues, it works best if learnt and acted out, but it can also be effective as a dramatised reading if you do not have time to learn it. The overall aim is for a meditative and serious feel.

Characters: MARY.

MARY: Kids! Who'd have 'em?

I suppose at one time or another all mothers have uttered those immortal words – but few, I'm sure, have ever really meant it! Even my own mother has said it a few times, usually when I've broken something, but never has she come closer to really meaning it than on the day I told her my extraordinary news. I mean, I've always wanted kids, ever since I can first remember playing with dolls, but even so, I wasn't planning on having one quite so soon. . .

Why would I? What's the big rush? Life was really good. I had a strong faith, a wonderful family and a new fiancé – a gorgeous local carpenter by the name of Joseph. Things were so good I would walk around with a permanent grin on my face. And things were about to get better, unbelievably better, but in a rather strange way.

One day, out of the blue, no appointment or anything, this angel appears. I know it sounds a bit far-fetched, but that's how it happened – no word of a lie. And this angel says to me that I'm pregnant, that I'm carrying God's own son – the promised Messiah – and that I should name him Jesus.

However unbelievable the story sounds, the most unbelievable thing is that not for one second did I doubt it. I don't want to sound all super-spiritual – I'm as human as the next person, with faults and foibles – but I *knew*, without a shadow of a doubt I knew. I asked how it was physically possible, which was explained, and then I said, 'I am the Lord's servant, and I am willing to do whatever he wants.' And I meant it.

After the initial adrenalin rush died down, it dawned on me that explaining the situation might not be so easy. My parents were shocked – there's no escaping it. They said they believed me – of course they would, they loved me dearly – but I could detect in their eyes a flicker of doubt. A fear of madness, maybe? I went to see my Aunt Elizabeth, who was also pregnant, and as soon as she caught sight of me she greeted me with 'Mother of my Lord!' How she knew I don't know, but I'm grateful that she did.

And then, of course, there was dear Joseph. Confused and fearful, he so wanted to believe. And if there was one person I needed to understand, it was him. Thankfully, the angel had the foresight to visit him too, and I knew that with Joseph by my side I could weather any storm – the storms of disapproval from my peers and townsfolk with their black looks and sly comments, and the storms of physical pain and exhaustion that would come with the circumstances of the birth, which are now so well known. But Joseph was there, every step of the way.

I won't bore you with all the details of the birth, but I will tell you something they never repeat. After eight days we took our child to the temple in Jerusalem, to present him to God, as was our custom. Then we named him Jesus and offered a sacrifice of two young pigeons and a pair of doves. In the temple courts we were met by an old man who took our child into his arms and said, 'My eyes have seen your salvation.' Joseph and I were both moved to tears as he spoke these words over our Jesus. But then, among other things, he said, 'A sword will pierce your own soul, too.' He looked at me, and there were tears in his eyes as well. 'A sword will pierce your own soul.'

Later, after we had completed everything required by the law, we returned to Galilee, to our home town of Nazareth. And here we remain. Jesus is fourteen now and has gained quite some reputation. He has incredible wisdom, far beyond his years, although I'm aware all mothers say that! And he has grown strong. He's his father's apprentice – my two carpenters – though secretly Joseph and I are sure he's destined for other, greater things.

Sometimes, when I'm on my own, I allow my thoughts to wander. And I think of that old man in Jerusalem and recall his words. 'A sword will pierce your own soul, too.' And I fear what they might mean. Still, I suppose this is the pain and privilege of motherhood.

Kids! Who'd have 'em?

I would. Every time, from the bottom of my heart, I would.

BIBLE REFERENCES
Luke 1:38, 2:34–5

It Takes Two to Tango

'It's my duty as a mother to give you a lecture, so sit back and listen'

INTRODUCTION

Imagine a family hearing the shocking news of their teenage daughter's pregnancy. Imagine the strain on those relationships, and add into that equation the innocence of the daughter. Sound familiar? This piece uses a modern family to help imagine the personal cost involved in the Bible account.

Characters: PAT; CLIVE; MARY.

CLIVE is sitting at a table reading the newspaper. PAT enters, excitedly reading a letter.

PAT: Oh, Clive, isn't it wonderful? I've had a lovely letter from my sister Elizabeth!

CLIVE: Oh, how spiffing.

PAT: Don't be like that – you like Elizabeth, don't you?

CLIVE: Well. . .

PAT: Don't be so silly, of course you do.

CLIVE: Anything you say, dear.

PAT: Good, 'cos I've invited her to stay for a while.

CLIVE: Oh no! What the dickens did you do that for, Pat?

PAT: You know full well why. What with her, um, 'condition', and Zach away with work for the next couple of weeks I thought she might need my sisterly support.

CLIVE: I thought you didn't agree with her having this baby.

PAT: Well, no, I admit it. I think at her age she's a bit past child-bearing. I mean, she's no spring chicken, is she?

CLIVE: She's younger than you are.

PAT: Watch it! Anyway, I think at times like this families should draw together.

CLIVE: What does she say in her letter, then?

PAT: Well, bless her, she says (*Reading*) 'I really don't want to get in the way and be a trial for you and Clive, so I don't think I should come.'

CLIVE: Oh good!

PAT: (*Continues reading*) 'But if it makes you feel better, Pat, I'll come.'

CLIVE: Oh no!

PAT: Stop moaning and read your paper.

(*MARY enters, looking nervous*)

PAT: Hello, love. Ooh, you look like you've seen a ghost! Sit down and have a cuppa.

MARY: Thanks.

CLIVE: You okay, love?

PAT: Course she is, Clive – stop interfering. Out till all hours with your boyfriend last night, were you?

MARY: He's got a name, Mum, and he's not my boyfriend – he's my fiancé.

PAT: Oh, excuse me, I keep forgetting he's your betrothed. Your dad's been getting all excited 'cos Auntie Elizabeth is coming to stay. I can't wait to be an Auntie.

MARY: And a grand– (*Stops herself*)

PAT: What was that, love?

MARY: Er. . . and a grand auntie you'll make, too.

PAT: Ah, thank you, love – isn't that sweet, Clive?

CLIVE: Eh?

PAT: Oh, forget it! Are you sure you're all right, Mary love?

MARY: Oh, I don't know. Look – I've got something to tell you both.

PAT: Oh yeah?

MARY: I think it might come as a bit of a shock.

CLIVE: This sounds ominous.

PAT: Clive, sshh!

MARY: I'm pregnant.

PAT: (*Pause*) No, you're confused, love – that's your Auntie Elizabeth.

MARY: I know it's hard to take in, but it's true. I am pregnant.

PAT: No! How could you be so stupid! Are you 100 per cent sure?

MARY: I've done one of those kits, but I had it on the highest authority anyway.

PAT: This isn't how I brought you up, is it? I gave you morals! You had so many morals they were coming out your ears!

MARY: But Mum –

PAT: Don't stop me mid-flow, Mary. It's my duty as a loving mother to give you a lecture, so sit back and listen.

MARY: But you don't know the facts.

PAT: Oh, I think I do. I'm a woman of the world. I know the facts of life. I know how these little mistakes happen. You young people, you've no respect, no idea of standards. You've broken your father's heart.

CLIVE: Eh?

PAT: See – speechless, he is!

MARY: Please listen to me.

PAT: Of course I blame Elizabeth. Getting in the family way at her age has put silly ideas into your head.

MARY: No, Mum.

CLIVE: Maybe we should just –

PAT: (*Interrupts*) Keep your nose out, Clive! If you can't say anything useful, best keep quiet. I suppose you'll expect me to look after the baby?

MARY: No.

PAT: I can see it now. Muggins with the sprog, up to her armpits in ploppy nappies, while you go gadding off night-clubbing with your boyfriend.

MARY: Fiancé!

PAT: *Fiancé!* You may be engaged, but you're supposed to wait until you're married. His mum will roast him over the coals when she hears.

MARY: It's not Joe's fault.

PAT: Not Joe's fault? Did you hear that, Clive?

CLIVE: Yes, dear.

PAT: Not his fault, my foot! I'm not letting you off the hook – it takes two to tango.

MARY: We didn't tango. Why can't you listen? Joe isn't the father.

PAT: (*Shocked pause*) But. . . but. . .

CLIVE: I think what your mother is trying to say is, if Joe isn't, then who is?

MARY: I think I'd better save that for another day.

PAT: You don't deserve to live under this roof. I wish – I wish I'd never had you!

MARY: Mum, please don't say that.

CLIVE: Stop it, Pat.

PAT: Shut up – I'll say my piece! My daughter, the neighbourhood good-time girl? It's not how it should be. Not how it's meant to be.

MARY: You'll never understand, Mum, because you never listen. What I've been trying to tell you all along is – I'm still a virgin. (*Shocked expressions as lights fade*)

BIBLE REFERENCE
Luke chapter 1

Christmas Baubles

'What a terrible thing to say! I may only be a bauble, but I do have feelings!'

INTRODUCTION

The effect of this sketch is somewhat improved if you can use three bald actors to play the baubles. However, swimming caps can be used as an alternative. If you can make some kind of prop so only the heads are visible, it will also add to the effectiveness.

Characters: RED; GOLD; GREY.

RED: Ooh, it's dark in here. (*Pause*) I said, it's dark in here.

GOLD: Yes, we heard you – change the record, why don't you!

RED: Calm down, moody!

GOLD: Well, that's all you've said for the past eleven months. It gets so boring.

RED: Well, excuse me for breathing. (*Pause*) 'Tis dark, though, innit?

GOLD: Right, that's it! I can't stand it any more. Let me out of here! Please, someone, let me out!

(*Effect of opening lid, either by removing cover on stage or a light change*)

RED: Blimey, it worked – they took the lid off!

GOLD: I should have tried that months ago.

RED: What's up with him?

GOLD: Heaven only knows.

RED: (*To GREY*) Oi, mate! You can wake up now. I said, you can wake up now!

GREY: (*Wakes with a start*) Aagghh!

GOLD: (*Startled*) Good grief, I nearly had a heart attack.

GREY: Oh look, the lid's been taken off.

GOLD: Ah, the penny drops.

GREY: Must be Christmas already. Comes round quick, doesn't it?

GOLD: (*Sarcastic*) Well, you've had such a busy time, haven't you?

GREY: Eh?

RED: Oh, don't listen to him! Just enjoy breathing fresh air into your lungs again. Go on, take a deep breath. (*ALL breathe in deeply*)

ALL: Ugghh!

RED: Oh, that is disgusting! She's been cooking again, hasn't she, the lady of the house. She's no Delia, is she?

GREY: Put the lid back on, mate, do us all a favour.

GOLD: Don't tempt fate, you silly idiot.

RED: It's her annual effort at the Christmas pudding – she's left it in far too long.

GREY: She needs a lighter touch with the suet.

GOLD: Hang on – what are you two talking about? You're baubles – you can't smell anything, you haven't got a nose!

RED: What a terrible thing to say! I may only be a bauble, but I do have feelings!

GREY: Yeah, we do have feelings.

GOLD: What a pair! However did I get stuck with you?

RED/GREY: Ooh!

RED: Here, what did you make of the fairy on top of the tree last year?

GREY: Yeah, bit of all right, wasn't she?

RED: You're not kidding she was! Wouldn't mind switching on *her* lights! (*Both laugh*) Mind you, I didn't get much of a view of her. I was stuck round the back of the tree on one of the bottom branches.

GREY: Yeah, me too.

RED: Where were you, then, golden boy?

GOLD: If you must know, I was on display front and central.

RED: (*Mimics*) 'I was on display front and central.' Well, bully for you.

GOLD: And you can both keep your eyes off Angela. She's far too high-brow for you two.

RED: Oh, he's on first-name terms with the fairy.

GOLD: Yes, well, Angela and I became very close last year. There was only a garland of tinsel and a chocolate Santa between us.

RED: Oh, how sweet.

GREY: Yeah, very sweet.

GOLD: Enough of the sarcasm. I'm just informing you in case you try to rise above your lowly stations.

RED: Rise above our stations! Listen, twonk-head, you only came out of a box like the rest of us.

GOLD: (*Affronted*) How dare you! I was never in a multi-pack. I was purchased and wrapped individually.

RED: Individually?

GREY: Individually?

GOLD: Yes, individually!

RED: And where were you bought from?

GOLD: Harrods.

RED: How much?

GOLD: £3.79.

RED: £3.79? Is that real gold, then?

GOLD: No, but I am hand-painted. And what about you, how much were you?

RED: Ninety-nine pence from Woolies.

GOLD: What, just for you?

RED: No, for a box of twelve. I'm the only one left. All the rest have come a cropper over the years – dropped, trodden on, attacked by their mangy old dog.

GOLD: And what about you?

GREY: Me? I was only five pence at a car-boot sale.

RED: And a bargain at twice the price.

GOLD: But where were you bought from originally?

GREY: I don't like to talk about it. (*Cries*) I've had a terrible life.

RED: Oh look, you've started him off now!

GOLD: Well, I didn't know he had a – history.

RED: It's all right, mate. Come on, stop crying or your paint will start running. They won't put you on the tree then, will they?

GOLD: Well, neither of you have got a hope this year, I'm afraid. Only true quality stands the test of time. They do have standards, you know. I think that only I will be gaining entrance to that fir-encrusted paradise.

RED: Ignore him! Delusions of grandeur. As long as you catch her eye, you're in, mate, trust me.

GREY: Hey, that's not on!

RED: What?

GREY: He's opening a present, and it ain't Christmas yet.

RED: That is outrageous! These humans have no patience, do they? No self-control!

GOLD: Wait a minute – it's not a present, it's a. . . it's a. . .

GREY: Yes, well, what is it?

RED: (*Gasps*) It's a box of flashing Christmas baubles!

GREY: So it is – and they match the tree.

RED: And the tinsel.

GOLD: And the fairy lights. Angela!

RED: Don't move! She's looking over!

GREY: (*Sneezes*)

GOLD: Don't move, you idiot!

GREY: Sorry, it's not my fault – those pine-cones play havoc with my sinuses.

RED: Oh no, he's picked up that lid again.

GREY: So he has, and he's heading this way.

GOLD: We're doomed! Doomed, I say – DOOMED!

(*The lid is replaced – either cover the baubles onstage or dim the lights*)

RED: It's dark in here.

GOLD: (*Groans*)

GREY: (*Pause*) I spy with my little eye something beginning with D.

RED: Er, dire situation?

GREY: Nope.

RED: Ooh – a dinosaur!

GREY: Nope.

RED: I've got it – darkness!

GREY: Yep!

GOLD: (*Groans*)

Easter

The Comforter

'Dear woman, here is your son'

INTRODUCTION

This monologue focuses on Jesus's request to John to comfort his mother. Meditative in its style, it is ideal for a reflective Easter service, and attempts to capture something of the hopelessness of Easter Saturday.

Character: JOHN.

JOHN: She's gone to sleep, finally. It's hard seeing someone like that – she was so vulnerable, so needy. All the time I've known her she's been the strong one, the quiet one, who seems to watch and understand everything. But tonight she was asking all the questions, and I didn't know what to say. She needs me to be strong – I've lost a friend, my best friend, but a mother losing her son, the boy she cared for. . . She kept on saying, 'Why, why did it have to be him?'

I feel so helpless trying to comfort her, when all I really want to do is to cry in her arms and have her tell me it's all going to be all right. But I must be strong. That was what Jesus said. I know he wanted me to look after his mum. His last words to me were, 'Here is your mother.' And he said to her, 'Here is your son.' He loved her and knew how much she'd be hurting, but also that she could comfort me. He was thinking of us to the last, even when he was suffering so much.

It's getting light. I've been up all night. Saturday now. The first Sabbath without him. So many people knew him. To some he was Lord and Messiah, healer, teacher, enemy of the state, even blasphemer. Sometimes I was confused, but at the end there, he reminded us who he was – family, best friend, son. And that's what we miss most. All this talk of bread of life, the Word, the King, even the Son of God – that means nothing right now. More important for me just now is that he was the son of Mary and the friend of John.

Did it have to happen? I'm so numb I can't make any sense of it, but he knew, didn't he? Or seemed to, anyway. This is the hour that he talked about when he was to become glorified. How? In what way is this 'glory'? In what way is this 'light'? All I see is darkness. Mary remembered his words, 'Now is your time of grief, but soon you will rejoice. . .' Rejoice. . . How can we do that? What I'm experiencing now is real, the bleakness of this morning, and the reality of his death. I saw it. I was there the whole time and I know he's gone.

I believed him. I saw his miracles. But this? He's been buried. How can I have faith, hope or rejoicing when faced with that? 'For a short time you will not see me,' he said. But when I asked him what that meant, he never told me straight, just said to trust. It was so easy to believe him when he was here. I trusted him, and when I didn't understand I still felt a sense of security that he knew what he was doing. Not so easy now.

Who was this man? I thought there was something between us. While others revered him I stayed close, like a brother, but there's still so much I didn't understand. Jesus, why couldn't we have had more time, grown old together? By asking me to look after Mary, I became part of your family, in a way. I loved you as my brother – did I ever tell you that?

Before Mary went to sleep, after she had calmed down, she seemed to click back briefly into the woman that I know, organised and thoughtful. She's decided to go to his tomb on Sunday – well, tomorrow now – to dress the body. Her friends will be there and it will be good for her. I know she refuses to believe that this is the end, but maybe by seeing the body again she can come to terms with what has happened. She'll see the tomb and understand the truth.

One of the things he said keeps coming back to me. 'Greater love has no man than this, that he lay down his life for his friends.' There was a reason he had to do it, and in dying he somehow showed us the greatest picture of love. I felt that more than anything when he spoke to Mary and me from the cross. Greater love has no man. . . There was a reason. This Saturday morning I can't even begin to comprehend what it was, but I will hold on. I know that he loved us and for that reason he died. Today I will continue to mourn for the loss of my best friend, and tomorrow – well, who knows. Tomorrow things may be different.

BIBLE REFERENCE
John chapter 19

Living Water

'I am thirsty'

INTRODUCTION

This meditation at the cross is from the point of view of a woman who observed Jesus's interaction with the woman at the well. She stands at a distance from the crucifixion and recalls how she stood at a distance in her previous encounter with Jesus, too.

Character: WOMAN.

WOMAN: Everyone was talking about this big execution – all my friends were, anyway. Some revolutionary, apparently, trying to cause trouble for the Romans and bring about the end of Judaism. Well, I was inquisitive, wasn't I? I like to be in the know. Besides, I wanted to find out what someone capable of these crimes looked like.

And as soon as I saw him, I knew I'd met him before. And I couldn't believe it was the same man that was hanging up there now.

I remember it very clearly, all those months ago, when this same man was at my local well, of all places. He didn't see me as he sat down to take a rest by the well. Nor, thankfully, did the woman coming to draw her water that he ended up speaking to. No, I stayed hidden. Which suited me fine – and it was a lucky thing, too, being as he's up there now. I don't

want to be seen mixing with criminals! As for the
woman he was talking to that day, well, I'm sorry, but
I do have standards, you know – and let's just say she
wasn't exactly the model wife!

Anyway, the whole thing happened about lunch-
time a couple of months ago, before all this execution
stuff. Usually I go to draw my water from the well first
thing in the morning and then again in the evening. All
we girls do – it's a bit of a social gathering, you might
say. We share any news, have a bit of a gossip – nothing too vicious, you understand – then off we all go. But
this particular morning, I'd had a bit of a nightmare. To
start with, my husband had had a bit of a heavy night
on the old grog, so had woken up like a bear with a sore
head. On top of that the kids were larking about, not
eating their breakfast, not getting packed for school. So,
what with all that, I didn't have the time or energy to
make it to the well. By the time I'd got everyone out the
house it was the best part of half-past eleven.

When I eventually approached the well, who did I
see crashed out by the side of it? None other than this
Jewish fella, Jesus, the same one who's about to be
killed. Now back then I'd heard a few stories about
him – word gets around, you know. Apparently he
was a bit of a one with his miracles and teachings.
Some people were really bowled over by him,
thought he was going to shake things up around here
a bit. Wonder where they all are now? Anyway, personally I didn't have an opinion. All I needed to know
was, I'm a Samaritan woman, and he's a Jewish man,
so best avoid him. So I hid behind a tree, thinking
he'll probably be on his way in a few minutes and I
can carry on. But no, he just sat there.

About ten minutes later who should turn up, rope

and bucket in hand, but that woman! I've no idea what her name is, but we girls used to call her the harlot. It might seem a bit strong, but we had it on very good authority from Betty that she had been married on numerous occasions.

She always used to come and draw water with the rest of us, first thing in the morning and then again in the evening, but we hadn't seen her for months. Some of the girls used to give her a lot of verbal abuse, so I figured she'd just decided to avoid the busy times – best thing all round, really. Anyway, there she was, bold as brass, walking up to the well, not a care in the world, and this Jesus sitting there, plain for all to see. So she just ignores him and starts drawing her own water, when all of a sudden he turns round and asks her for a drink! Well, you should have seen the look on her face. A Jewish man, lowering himself to talk to a Samaritan woman – it was quite simply unheard of. But she got over the shock – she's a natural with men – and gave him some water.

Next thing, Jesus starts telling her something about giving her living water. Well, I don't know anything about living water – things living in it, maybe, what with the state of that well. But he went on to say that this water was a 'perpetual spring within you, watering you forever with eternal life'. At that point he lost me. I never was the sharpest tool in the box, but the harlot was hanging on to his every word. I don't know how he was going to get this special water – he didn't have a bucket. Another one of his miracles, no doubt! Not working so well now, though, are they? He said to her, 'You shall never thirst again.' But just now, up there on the cross I heard him say he was thirsty. Ironic, really, poor bloke.

And of course the harlot was desperate for this living water. Who wouldn't be, if it saved you traipsing to the well day in, day out. He went on to tell her how we could all worship God, Jew and Samaritan alike. I bet that's one of the reasons he upset so many people. He said that the Messiah would come and explain everything, and for his grand finale announced he was that Messiah. I ask you! It's sad, really. He's just a man, after all, a man who's thirsty and needs a drink. You know, when he was there, chattering with that woman, I thought to myself, if she can talk to him, so can I. She went running off to tell everyone that she had met the Messiah, but I just stayed there. Frozen. Wish I'd spoken to him now.

It doesn't seem right, him being up there. He didn't seem like a bad man – in fact, very gentle. Much nicer than we ever were to that woman. . .

BIBLE REFERENCE
John 4:1–15

Funeral Supplies

'You did dress the body, I hope? It'll stink to high heaven otherwise!'

INTRODUCTION

This is a three-hander sketch set in a funeral supplies store. Death and burial being what they are, it's hardly usual to have products brought back for a refund, but in the case of a miraculous resurrection things can get a touch confusing!

Characters: GEORGE; ARTHUR; MARY.

GEORGE: Hello? You here, Arthur?

ARTHUR: (*Offstage*) Yeah, hang on. With you in a second.

GEORGE: Take your time, my friend, no rush. (*Fiddles with items on counter, blows into a jar and a dusty substance billows out*) Oh, blast!

ARTHUR: (*Enters*) Sorry, George – just taking in a delivery.

GEORGE: No problem. Skinny latte for you, tall mocha for me.

ARTHUR: Ooh, you're a legend.

GEORGE: Service with a smile, my friend. So, business is good at the mo, is it?

ARTHUR: You're not kidding. Rushed off my feet, I am. Might have to take on extra staff.

GEORGE: Very nice too. Why the sudden upturn, then?

ARTHUR: Who knows, George, who knows? But dropping like flies, they are, dropping like flies. Must be the time of year.

GEORGE: Either that or our beloved Roman occupiers' habit of condemning people to grisly deaths for questionable crimes.

ARTHUR: Yeah, well, that too. In any case I'm not complaining. Where do people first stop when their loved ones pop their mortal clogs? Arthur and Jean's Funeral Supplies!

GEORGE: Everything you need to send your loved ones off in style and all under one roof.

ARTHUR: Precisely. Here, have a gander at that – the latest line in burial shrouds. Finest Egyptian linen. You won't find that in Argos. Feel the quality.

GEORGE: Very nice, Arthur.

ARTHUR: I can cut you a deal if you're interested.

GEORGE: No, I've told my missus she can just wrap me up in my old housecoat. I don't want any of this old rubbish.

ARTHUR: Oi, don't you let my Jean hear you say that!

GEORGE: Where is the old dragon, anyhow?

ARTHUR: Oh, hobnobbing with the great and the good. She got invited to a tea party hosted by Governor Pilate's missus.

GEORGE: Lady Procula! How did she wangle that?

ARTHUR: Well, it's a bit of a long story, but her ladyship consulted us after the sad demise of her pet poodle, Frisky.

GEORGE: Ah, poor Frisky. How did that happen?

ARTHUR: A bust of Caesar toppled over in their courtyard and – splat! Anyhow, Jean managed to get this very rare urn from Syria, and her ladyship is delighted.

GEORGE: What, this thing here? (*Points to the jar he blew in earlier*)

ARTHUR: Yep, the very one.

GEORGE: And where is Frisky now?

ARTHUR: In there! So don't touch it. Messing with Frisky is a crime worthy of execution.

GEORGE: Execution? Well, I'd better be on my way, Arthur.

ARTHUR: What? You haven't finished your mocha yet.

GEORGE: No, I need to get on – things to do, places to be! (*Charges out and bumps into MARY as she enters*) Oh, excuse me, madam.

MARY: Quite all right.

ARTHUR: A very warm welcome to you, madam, and how may I be of service this bright spring morning?

MARY: Well, it's a rather strange situation, really.

ARTHUR: Yes, bereavement does have the power to confuse and confound, does it not? Have you recently lost a loved one?

MARY: Yes. I mean, no. Well, sort of.

ARTHUR: Mmm, would you like a seat, madam – a glass of water, perhaps?

MARY: No, thank you.

ARTHUR: A mocha then?

MARY: No, I'm fine, thank you.

ARTHUR: I know it's a hard time, madam, but rest assured that here at Arthur and Jean's Funeral Supplies we can ensure that your loved one goes to the other side fully equipped and in true style.

MARY: It's a bit late for that, I'm afraid.

ARTHUR: Oh? Already had the funeral, have you?

MARY: Well, sort of.

ARTHUR: Sort of? You do seem rather vague, madam. What exactly is it I can do for you?

MARY: Well, to be honest I've come in for a cash refund.

ARTHUR: A refund? For what?

MARY: This. (*Plonks jar on counter*) It's a jar of your finest burial spices.

ARTHUR: Indeed it is, prepared with my secret mix of herbs and spices. Is there some problem with the product?

MARY: No, it's not that. It's just – how shall I put it – surplus to requirements.

ARTHUR: This is most irregular. How many jars did you pur-
chase?

MARY: Just the one.

ARTHUR: But it's unopened. You did dress the body, I hope? It'll
stink to high heaven otherwise!

MARY: Well, as it turned out, he's not actually dead.

ARTHUR: Not dead? So why did you buy burial spices?

MARY: Well, he was dead.

ARTHUR: And now he's. . . not?

MARY: No, he's still with us.

ARTHUR: Oh, I see. Yes, well, I'm sure his spirit is still with us,
madam, but his bodily remains should still be
attended to for hygiene's sake.

MARY: No, you don't understand. His body was placed in a
tomb, dead. After three days I went to apply your
finest burial spices and the body was gone.

ARTHUR: Well, that's just plain silly. Where had he gone to, for
pity's sake?

MARY: As a matter of fact, he'd gone for a little wander in the
garden.

ARTHUR: Oh, how nice, a wander round the garden! And how
would you know that?

MARY: Funny you should ask that. I bumped into him.

ARTHUR: Why am I not surprised. Well, madam, all I can say is
I've heard some far-fetched tales from people wanting
a refund, but this just about takes the biscuit.

MARY: It happens to be true.

ARTHUR: That's as may be, but I'm afraid we have a very strict
no-refunds policy.

MARY: Well, what am I going to do with a jar of burial spices?

ARTHUR: That's your problem. But I will say that they do make
a very pleasing potpourri.

MARY: You can't have potpourri in a jam jar, you silly fool!

ARTHUR: Wait a minute – I may have a suitable receptacle.

MARY: (*Spots Syrian urn and empties it on counter*) Here – this'll
           do.
ARTHUR: (*Gasps*) Frisky!
MARY: I beg your pardon?
ARTHUR: What have you done to Frisky?
MARY: I'm sorry, I'm not with you.
ARTHUR: Just put it down, put it down! Here, have a refund.
MARY: But I thought you had a strict policy.
ARTHUR: I've changed it, now just go away!
MARY: Well, if you're sure, thanks. Goodbye. (*Exits*)
ARTHUR: (*Scrapes Frisky back in urn*) Sorry, Frisky, but not a
           word, eh? Not a word. . .

BIBLE REFERENCE
Luke 24:1

The Road Sweepers

'I reckon we'll be hearing more of this Jesus of Nazareth'

INTRODUCTION

It might seem a little bit strange, but in all the joy of Palm Sunday and the great arrival have you ever spared a thought for the poor road sweepers who had to clear up all the crowd's mess? Interesting that this same crowd were the ones hurling insults at Jesus and calling for him to be crucified – hence its inclusion here in this Easter selection.

Characters: HAROLD; BOB.

HAROLD: Oh, look at that, will you? It's unbelievable, innit! I tell you, some people have no dignity, no decorum! It's enough to make you lose faith in the human race.

BOB: Well, we'd better get on. It won't clear itself up.

HAROLD: I could have been a computer engineer, you know. Oh yes, my teacher said to me, 'Harold, you know what you could be?' 'What?' I said. 'A computer engineer,' she said. But there you go. I weighed up my options, mulled it over and deliberated, but in the end I opted for road sweeping. Well, I thought, it's less taxing on the brain. But on days like this I rue the day, I tell you I do.

BOB: Well, it certainly has its ups and downs.

HAROLD: What's been going on, anyway? It looks like Jerusalem's answer to the Mardi Gras.

BOB: Oh, some bigwig rolled into town yesterday, and all
            the crowd got a bit overexcited.

HAROLD: Overexcited? That's an understatement – looks like
            they've been going about in a rampaging heathen
            throng.

BOB: Ooh no, I doubt that, Harold. There was a real chill in
            the air last night.

HAROLD: (*Pause*) What?

BOB: There was a real chill. It would have been far too cold
            to be wearing a thong.

HAROLD: Not a thong, you dopey lard – a *throng*, as in 'a large
            group'.

BOB: Oh.

HAROLD: I dunno, sometimes I worry about you. Hello, looks
            like someone's left their cloak behind.

BOB: Yeah, apparently they were all laying their cloaks on
            the ground as he came swanning in.

HAROLD: I've heard everything now. Look at it all – cloaks,
            branches, palm leaves, old tubes of Pringles, lumps of
            pooh, crisp wrappers. . . (*Suddenly stops*) Oh, how dis-
            gusting! Why on earth are there lumps of pooh all
            over the place?

BOB: Looks like donkey pooh.

HAROLD: Expert, are you?

BOB: I'd heard the bigwig arrived on a donkey. There's the
            evidence.

HAROLD: Very understated. All that crowd cheering and he rolls
            up on a donkey – a frightened donkey, at that!

BOB: Sounds strange, but it's what I heard.

HAROLD: Well, it's an interesting PR exercise, I suppose.

BOB: All been prophesied, apparently.

HAROLD: Oh, don't give me any of that hocus pocus. I've had it
            up to my ears with miracle workers and prophets.

BOB: 'Hosanna,' they were yelling. 'Hosanna to the Son of

David!'

HAROLD: Okay, Bob, calm yourself down.

BOB: 'Who is he?' some cried. 'Jesus of Nazareth,' replied others.

HAROLD: Yeah, well, whatever. We've had them all. Today's headline is tomorrow's chip wrappers.

BOB: Oh, I think you're wrong there, Harold. This was something a bit special. I reckon we'll be hearing more of this Jesus of Nazareth.

HAROLD: Something special, my foot! The yobs round here scream at anything. Remember that pop band McFly? One minute they're screaming their lungs out, the next no one's heard of them.

BOB: Oh, he'll last a bit longer than McFly, Harold.

HAROLD: We'll see, my son, we'll see. But I bet you his popularity won't last. Just mark my words.

BIBLE REFERENCE
John 12:12–19

A Ghostly Tale

'No, the whole ghostly realm was never my bag, but of course that was up to the point when I actually came face to face with one for myself. . .'

INTRODUCTION

Here is the first of two monologues from Peter's perspective, the first from Luke's account and the second from John's Gospel.

Character: PETER.

PETER: I've never been one for those soppy ghost stories. Load of rubbish, as far as I was concerned – ghouls and spectres. The whole lot of 'em go way beyond the scope of rational belief. It's just for kids, I thought. Mind you, even as a kid I was never taken in by them. No, my mum used to tuck me in at night with a lovely Enid Blyton story, every night, and I was as happy as Larry.

   No, the whole ghostly realm was never my bag, but of course that was up to the point when I actually came face to face with one for myself – a ghost, that is. Or at least I thought I did.

   It all occurred back in Jerusalem. Some of the other boys and I were chatting away, wondering what to do after the death of our master. We'd been kicking our heels a bit, if the truth be known, scared stiff of what would happen to us if anyone worked out we were part of Jesus' gang. Then we came across this funny old couple from some dump of a place called Emmaus. They told us this far-fetched tale about having had a private face-to-face meeting with – you'll never guess who – Jesus! Yeah, apparently he went on a lovely little stroll with them, then sat down and did a bit of a Bible study, stayed for tea – then, whoosh! Without a word of notice he disappeared into thin air. Well, call me cynical but the whole thing didn't strike me as being highly likely. I'm sure you would have reached the same conclusion yourselves.

But looking back on it now, with the benefit of hindsight, I really should have put two and two together. You see, not so long before I'd been down at the tomb, where they'd buried the master. I was with the two Marys, and Jesus' body – well, it had just disappeared into thin air. I went home, my head spinning, wondering what could possibly have happened, trying to fathom it all out. Come on – it's not rocket science, is it?

And it was while this dopey old couple from Emmaus were regaling us with their far-fetched tale that I was confronted with this ghostly entity! I screamed 'Aagghh!' You would have, too – be honest! In actual fact I nearly wet myself on the spot, and it's been a good number of years since I did that.

'Peace be with you,' it says. Peace, I thought! Not the first word that would leap to mind under those circumstances. Fear, maybe, or heart attack – but the last thing I felt at that particular moment was peaceful.

'Why are you troubled?' he says. Ooh, I wonder why, I thought to myself.

'Why do you doubt? Look at my hands. Look at my feet. Touch me. A ghost has no flesh and bones, as you can see I have.' And he did have flesh and bones.

Then he said it, what I knew deep down – 'It is I, myself.' Then it all fell into place – well, sort of. It wasn't a ghost, even if he did have the ability to walk through walls. It was the Master. The empty tomb, the odd couple's report – it all made sense, in a nonsensical kind of way.

Well, we all looked at each other, not sure whether to jump for joy or run into the street screaming for help. And then he said the strangest thing I've ever heard – 'Do you have anything to eat?' Can you believe it? So strangely human. I mean, who would think of eating at a time like that? And I love my food, don't get me wrong. Breakfast is my favourite meal. Oh yes, I'm a believer in the full works. Not much of a black-pudding man, though – pigs' blood doesn't agree with my constitution, or religion for that matter. But this particular day we were a bit short in the store cupboard. All we had kicking around was this mangy-looking bit of broiled fish. But he jumped at it. Ate it so quickly I don't think it hit the sides. And it was while he was eating that the whole thing suddenly seemed so obvious. Like, how could we have missed it before?

He started preaching to us, explaining the Scriptures – how he had to suffer, die and rise from the dead after three days. And how, because of this, repentance and forgiveness of sins would be made available and preached to all the nations, beginning here in Jerusalem. Of course he'd told us all this before, thousands of times, but somehow it never quite sank in, not until now.

He told us we were the witnesses, the ones with first-hand experience, so to speak – of his life, his mission, the revelation of who he was. And with that privilege came responsibility – a responsibility to tell others. The thought of this excited me, to a point, but it filled me with fear, too.

Still, he's given us a brief reprieve. We've got to stay in the city for a bit, to be equipped, to be 'clothed with power from on high'. Sounds fantastical, I know, but I have no room left for doubts, not any more. When I get it, this power, I'm gonna use it. Oh yeah! To the best of my God-given ability I'm gonna use it.

BIBLE REFERENCE
Luke 24:36–49

Breakfast with Jesus

'Do you love me?'

INTRODUCTION

This is a slightly different slant on Peter's story, from John's Gospel.

Character: PETER.

PETER: Unbelievable! Jesus was alive! Yes – it was more than we could ever have wished for. Our leader, the guy whom we left everything to follow, had risen from the dead! We saw him, dead and buried, and just a week later he was appearing all over the place in the flesh. And let me tell you – we were loving it! Well, everyone, that is, except me. Most of us have seen him now, and Thomas has actually spoken to him, shaken his hand – but me? Well, you know what I did before he died. Peter the rock, the trusted one, denied him. Swore he never knew the man, three times. So here was this guy who trusted me with everything, who knew I had denied him, and suddenly he's back, right as rain. I didn't know what to feel. I was so happy he was alive – don't get me wrong – but how on earth could I face him?

Anyway, this was all too much for me to deal with, and there was only one thing for it – leave the boys to their celebrating and go for an all-night fishing trip. Any time I've been up against it in the past, that's always sorted me out. Just me, the boat, the moon and a bunch of accommodating sea creatures. But when I announce this to the lads, what do they do?

'We'll come!' they say. Bringing their merry little party to my boat, when all I wanted was to be alone. But what could I do? You can't say no to your mates, can you?

So off we go, and I spend all night waiting by my nets, trying to ignore the others, who quite frankly couldn't give a monkey's about the fishing – they're just laughing and joking and banging on about the one thing I wish they wouldn't. And of course, when things are going badly, there's no stopping them getting worse. I caught nothing, not a single fish to be found in the whole useless pond!

Now, if there's one thing that gets up my nostrils, it's someone telling me how to do my job. And yep, you've guessed it, that's what happened next. Now I may not be the Jerusalem angler of the year, but I know my stuff, much better than some character on the shore telling me where to cast my nets. I was just about to give him a mouthful when John pipes up. 'It's him, the Messiah! He's on the beach.' And he was.

This was my chance. I had to speak to him and it had to be alone. I wanted to explain myself, tell him how sorry I was. And it was this manic impulse that carried me out of the boat and into the water before I really knew what was happening. So there I was, up to my waist in water, when I realised that it was some distance to the shore, and I really should have slipped off my new, open-toed sandals before descending into those murky depths. As I half-swam, half-waded to the beach, the boat predictably passed by me effortlessly. By the time I got to the master, the rest of the boys were all gathered round him like a bunch of admiring schoolgirls. And then I rolled up – disgraced, soaking wet and utterly miserable.

Jesus had cooked breakfast for us, though. Normally I love breakfast, but on this particular day I couldn't eat a sprat. It was awful. My nerves were jangling, I was consumed with guilt and I knew we needed to talk.

Finally, with an empty stomach and a load of seaweed stuck in my hair, the moment came. Jesus called me over and we left the group behind. It was wonderful and terrible all at the same time. I felt like a kid about to get a right rollicking – knowing I deserved it, but just not wanting to hear it.

He asked me if I loved him. Three times. 'Yes Lord, you know that I love you.' We both knew the significance of that number – three. And every time I answered him I heard my words of denial, 'I swear I never met the man.' I felt his disappointment, which was almost too much for me to bear, but I also had the feeling of being forgiven, completely.

Now, I'm not a crying man, but I did then – the Messiah had decided that I deserved another chance. What a gift – forgiveness from Jesus! The worst day of my life turned into the best. And then it was on with his work – but not until I'd grabbed a quick kipper from the fire. . .

BIBLE REFERENCE
John chapter 21

The Linen Store

'Little tear? I think you misunderstand. The whole thing's been torn in two!'

INTRODUCTION

The image of the temple curtain being torn in two from top to bottom is a powerful and evocative one. The immediate effect must have been far-reaching, and I wonder if any attempt was made to fix it. Of course, in reality some things are beyond stitching up. . .

Characters: BETTY; HENRY; JOSEPH.

BETTY is singing to herself, cutting some cloth. HENRY charges in.

HENRY: Disaster!

BETTY: I beg your pardon?

HENRY: Pure, unmitigated disaster!

BETTY: What are you on about, dearie?

HENRY: This! Look! Totally ruined.

BETTY: Oh, I'm sure it's not that bad. Calm yourself down and tell Betty all about it.

HENRY: Well, it's the curtain – look, it's torn! It's a total disaster.

BETTY: Oh, is that all? A torn curtain? I'll have that sorted in no time.

HENRY: It's not just any curtain. It's *the* curtain.

BETTY: Eh?

HENRY: The temple curtain. The curtain to the holy of holies.

BETTY: Ooh, I thought it looked like good quality. That's lovely
          cloth you've got there. Who are you, anyway?

HENRY: Oh, I'm no one, I've just been sent here by the High
          Priest. Your services come with the highest recommen-
          dation. Apparently you did the interiors for his sister's
          mansion.

BETTY: It's nice to hear I've got a good reputation.

HENRY: Well, that reputation is on the line. We need this
          repaired as quickly as possible. The High Priest is
          depending on you.

BETTY: Let's have a see, then. Where is this little tear?

HENRY: Little tear? I think you've misunderstood. The whole
          thing's been torn in two!

BETTY: Torn in two?

HENRY: Yes, from the top right the way down to the bottom.

BETTY: How on earth did you manage that? Having a priestly
          rave-up, were you?

HENRY: No, we were not! It just – well, it just sort of happened.

BETTY: Likely story – not your fault, of course.

HENRY: I can assure you it's not down to our negligence.

BETTY: Whatever. But I'm telling you, it would take someone
          with Samson-like strength to rip material of that qual-
          ity.

HENRY: Look, I can't explain it any further. When can you have
          it fixed?

BETTY: Well, I'll have a look today, dearie, but if it's as bad as
          you say it may be beyond repair.

HENRY: Beyond repair? Do you not realise the importance of
          this curtain?

BETTY: That's as may be, but I know my furnishings, and some-
          times things are, well, impossible to fix.

HENRY: I'll be back in two hours to check on your progress. Please
          do your utmost – the High Priest is counting on you.

BETTY: I'll do whatever I can.

HENRY: (*Charges out as JOSEPH enters*) Excuse me.

JOSEPH: Hello, Betty.

BETTY: Hello, Joseph, love.

JOSEPH: He's in a bit of a rush.

BETTY: Priestly duties, dear. Now, what can I do for you?

JOSEPH: I need some cloth.

BETTY: How about this? The old temple curtain, torn in two. I'm pretty sure it's beyond repair.

JOSEPH: Nah, a bit too ornate for what I need. I just need a simple burial cloth.

BETTY: Oh, I'm sorry, Joseph, love – you lost someone close?

JOSEPH: Sort of, yeah. A very good friend.

BETTY: Anyone I know?

JOSEPH: Probably – Jesus of Nazareth.

BETTY: Oh, I heard they were executing him today. I didn't know you were friends.

JOSEPH: Well, it was only recently. He's had quite an effect on me, and what with that travesty of a trial I thought I could at least sort out a decent burial.

BETTY: Will they let you have his body, then?

JOSEPH: I've got to get permission from Pilate. Don't see a problem. I've got the tomb – just need a cloth.

BETTY: How about some Egyptian silk?

JOSEPH: Too flashy. Something simple.

BETTY: Some linen?

JOSEPH: Perfect. How much?

BETTY: It costs next to nothing – take it for free, and let me know how it goes with Pilate.

JOSEPH: I will. Thanks, Betty. (*JOSEPH exits*)

BETTY: (*Pause*) Now, let's look at this curtain. Good for nothing, I'll wager. Absolutely good for nothing!

BIBLE REFERENCE
Matthew 27:45–56

Old Testament

Creature Comforts

'Would you credit it! Even a cup of water's out of the question. In Egypt, the water ran like streams'

INTRODUCTION

The Old Testament contains stories so rich and dramatic, I hope you enjoy this short selection and have fun in performing them. We begin with those moaning minnies that Moses had to put up with wandering around in the desert.

Characters: ROGER; MILDRED.

ROGER and MILDRED are lying down under a blanket. ROGER is fidgeting.

ROGER: Oh, this is ridiculous. (*Sighs deeply*) Are you awake, Mildred? (*Pause*) Mildred, are you awake?

MILDRED: Yes! Of course I am – how can I sleep with you wriggling about all over the place?

ROGER: Well, it's not my fault. I can't get comfortable, can I?

MILDRED: Move then, for goodness' sake, and find a new spot.

ROGER: (*Moves about*) Oooh, ow!

MILDRED: What now?

ROGER: I've just sat on a jaggedy rock. Ooh, it's got me right on the coccyx.

MILDRED: Oh, I give up.

ROGER: Just my luck, innit. In the middle of the desert and I manage to sit on the one solitary rock in the whole place.

MILDRED: Keep it down, Roger – you'll wake the whole place up.

ROGER: Well, I don't know how anyone can sleep, really I don't. I've got sand in the bottom of my sleeping bag again.

MILDRED: Well, you should be more careful with it.

ROGER: I am careful! This sleeping bag hasn't been outside this tent and I've still got half the bloomin' Sahara in the bottom of it.

MILDRED: Empty it out, then, for pity's sake.

ROGER: That's one thing you could say about Egypt. I know it wasn't perfect, but at least there wasn't sand as far as the eye can see.

MILDRED: No, not where we were, carting rocks about to build pyramids all day.

ROGER: Oh, what I wouldn't give to be back there now! Bliss, it was, compared with this purgatory. Why did we listen to him?

MILDRED: Just settle down and make the most of it, won't you?

ROGER: I'm absolutely parched. My throat is as dry as a bone. Is there any water, Mildred?

MILDRED: No, you knocked the last of it over when you were fidgeting.

ROGER: Would you credit it! Even a cup of water's out of the question. In Egypt, the water ran like streams.

MILDRED: Yeah, like it did when we were down in Elim – you forgotten the twelve springs and seventy palm trees?

ROGER: That was over a week ago, love. Now we're back to scraping about for everything.

MILDRED: Some people are never satisfied.

ROGER: And what about just before Elim, in the Desert of Shur? We didn't drink for three days. Three days! I'm surprised I didn't drop down dead.

MILDRED: Yeah, pity, that. At least I would have had some peace and quiet.

ROGER: Charming! Then we had to put up with that bitter stuff at Marah. Oh, why didn't we stay put in Egypt?

MILDRED: Er, I think it had something to do with shackles and slavery!

ROGER: Well, apart from that.

MILDRED: Let's see. Oh yeah, how about frogs and locusts and rivers of blood?

ROGER: All right, all right. I grant you it wasn't perfect, but at least we had some dignity.

MILDRED: Dignity? Oh Roger, you must be joking.

ROGER: Well, maybe not dignity, but we knew where we stood, at least. Things were set out for us, organised. We knew where our next meal was coming from.

MILDRED: We get food here too.

ROGER: In a manner of speaking.

MILDRED: What about all that meat yesterday? Some kind of miracle, wouldn't you say?

ROGER: Well, if it had been roast beef, maybe, or lamb – doner kebab, even – but quail!

MILDRED: You're just too flipping fussy.

ROGER: I know we were starving, but I do have standards, love. Quail? Ugghh! Back in Egypt we never had quail. We got cheese on toast, spaghetti hoops, chilli con carne. . .

MILDRED: We got no such thing, Roger – a plate of gruel if we were lucky.

ROGER: Well, at least that's better than quail.

MILDRED: And what about the manna?

ROGER: The what?

MILDRED: The manna! Bread from heaven, fresh every day.

ROGER: Huh! How long will that last?

MILDRED: Well, Moses has told us God will provide, every day, and he has not let us down so far.

ROGER: All this talk of food's made me hungry. Do you fancy a midnight snack?

MILDRED: You know the manna doesn't come until first thing in the morning. You'll have to be patient.

ROGER: Forget that – I hid a bit away earlier!

MILDRED: Roger! We were specifically told not to do that.

ROGER: Well, rules are supposed to be bent a little bit. Now, do you want any or not?

MILDRED: Oh, go on then. It's best we get rid of the evidence.

ROGER: (Digs out bread) Oh! Ugghh! That is revolting!

MILDRED: Oh, what now?

ROGER: It's got maggots crawling all over it.

MILDRED: You're kidding!

ROGER: No, look!

MILDRED: Well, don't wave it about over here! I don't want a load of maggots in my sleeping bag.

ROGER: That's just about the limit. I think we should call it a day and head back to the creature comforts of Egypt.

MILDRED: You just don't get it, do you?

ROGER: Get what?

MILDRED: We're heading towards the promised land. Away from slavery and persecution. The place God has prepared for us, the place previous generations longed for.

ROGER: Yeah, and look where all that longing's got us. Sand, maggots and jaggedy rocks!

MILDRED: Roger, we're heading towards our destiny, our birthright, and you're gonna chuck it all in at the first bit of discomfort – go back to Egypt and slavery, tail between your legs.

ROGER: But we knew where we stood, everything was in order, in its place, we were safe.

MILDRED: I don't want to be safe any more. You're like a pig, Roger.

ROGER: Pardon?

MILDRED: A pig satisfied to be swilling around in his own mess when, just beyond the horizon, over a few obstacles, is a five-star piggy hotel, fit for a king. He just needs courage and faith.

ROGER: Oh, is that all?

MILDRED: So what are you then – a man earnestly seeking his destiny or an easily satisfied pig?

ROGER: (*Pause*) Be morning soon. Give it an hour or so and dawn will be rising. I'll go and fetch us some nice fresh manna, find us some water. I'll come back and do you breakfast in bed. How does that sound?

MILDRED: Nice. It sounds really nice. (*Lights fade. Morning sound effects*)

BIBLE REFERENCE
Exodus 15:22–16:26

The Noise the Unicorn Made

'How do you do? I'm building an ark and everyone thinks I'm a nutter!'

INTRODUCTION

I wrote this a few years ago, and it's gone through a couple of changes over time – to remove the cornier jokes, if the truth be known! All the characters are seated, rising to deliver their lines, with the exception of the Narrator, who holds the piece together. As Noah tries to woo various species onto the ark, the question is, who will trust him?

Characters: NARRATOR; NOAH; ULYSSES THE UNICORN; CARLA THE COW; DILYS THE DUCK.

All characters are seated in a line, except the NARRATOR, who stands to one side.

NARR: Many, many moons ago, at the dawn of time, there was a man, and his name was Noah.

NOAH: How do you do? I'm building an ark and everyone thinks I'm a nutter!

NARR: God had personally asked Noah to build an ark and had given instructions to fill it with all kinds of creatures. So, ladies and gentlemen, for your enjoyment we have enlisted the help of some of those characters, now played by actors, to illustrate our story. Joining Noah. . .

NOAH: How do you do? I'm building an ark and everyone thinks I'm a nutter!

NARR: We have Carla the cow. . .

CARLA: Moo.

NARR: Dilys the duck. . .

DILYS: Quack.

NARR: And Ulysses the unicorn.

ULYSSES: (*Puzzled look*) Psst! Psst!

NARR: Yes?

ULYSSES: What noise do I make?

NARR: I beg your pardon?

ULYSSES: What noise do I make?

NARR: Well, I don't know, you're supposed to be the unicorn.

ULYSSES: That's as may be, but I don't know what noise I'm supposed to make.

NARR: Well, just make one up, for goodness' sake!

ULYSSES: Make one up?

NARR: Yes! Improvise. I'll cue you back in. Joining Noah. . .

NOAH: How do you do? I'm building an ark and everyone thinks I'm a nutter!

NARR: We have Carla the cow. . .

CARLA: Moo.

NARR: Dilys the duck. . .

DILYS: Quack.

NARR: And Ulysses the unicorn.

ULYSSES: (*Strange strangulated noise*)

NARR: Is that the best you can do?

ULYSSES: Do you want to switch parts?

NARR: No. I suppose it will have to do. So, Noah's strange ark-building project, miles away from any water, was getting confused reactions from the locals.

CARLA: He's a nutter.

DILYS: He's a nutter.

ULYSSES: He's a nutter.

NOAH: Everyone thinks I'm a nutter.

NARR: But Noah was not to be discouraged. He was determined to fill the ark with all creatures, as God
instructed. He started his mission with Carla the cow.

CARLA: Moo, this ark-building project does seem rather doo-
lally.

NOAH: Yes, but there is a perfectly rational explanation.

NARR: Noah explained in great detail his obedience to God's
plan, and Carla listened with an open mind. (*CARLA
mimes listening and gives an excited moo*)

NOAH: In addition to this, if you agree to join today I can still
fix you up with one of the luxury upper-deck cabins
with sea views and access to the cocktail bar.

NARR: Carla excitedly agreed.

CARLA: MOO!

NARR: Noah's next customer, however, took a little more per-
suading. It was understandable for there to be some
apprehension from Dilys the duck.

DILYS: Quack.

NOAH: It is absolutely vital to the survival of your species to
come aboard.

DILYS: Why?

NOAH: Well, as I've been trying to explain, there's going to be
the most dreadful flood – towns, countries, continents
will be swept away.

DILYS: I don't want to appear ungrateful, Noah, but I can
swim.

NOAH: (*Pause*) Oh, I see your point.

DILYS: Call me a fool, but a flood doesn't really fill me with
dread, like it would a cow (*CARLA moos*) or a unicorn
(*ULYSSES makes noise*).

NOAH: Look, I know this might sound crazy, especially to
you. I don't claim to understand it, but all I know is
that this ark is the only refuge. Maybe the rain will be

so torrential for so long, you won't physically be able to stand it. Maybe the waters will become polluted. I don't know, but I do know the ark will be the only escape.

NARR: Noah's heartfelt speech sent a tear rolling down Dilys's beak, so she agreed to join up. A much tougher proposition was Ulysses the unicorn.

ULYSSES: (*Strangulated noise*) I've never heard anything so utterly ridiculous in my life!

NOAH: Which bit is ridiculous?

ULYSSES: All of it! A flood that's going to wipe out life as we know it! It hardly seems likely, does it?

NOAH: It may seem unlikely, but I promise you it will happen.

ULYSSES: So you say. A dotty old crackpot with senile dementia. But of course the weather forecasters don't agree, do they?

NOAH: Well, they never get it right.

ULYSSES: Maybe not, but look at that ark.

NOAH: What about it?

ULYSSES: Not exactly the QE2, is it?

NOAH: It's been built to precise specifications as instructed.

ULYSSES: Instructed by whom?

NOAH: God.

ULYSSES: God? What did he do, fax you the blueprint?

NOAH: No, not exactly, it's too complicated to explain, but if you don't come on board, your species will be wiped out.

ULYSSES: Well, Noah, I'd love to come with you, I really would. But I know for a fact the missus won't go for it.

NOAH: Can't you persuade her?

ULYSSES: If you knew my wife, you'd know you can't persuade her about anything. No, she's very particular about her mode of transportation, and I don't think your rickety old ark will pass her stringent safety tests. Sorry, but what can I do?

NOAH: Well, if you change your mind you know where to find me.

ULYSSES: With that outside your house everyone knows where to find you! (*Laughs*)

NARR: However hard Noah tried, he could do nothing to persuade Ulysses to come aboard. Then, one day. . .

NOAH: (*Holds out hand*) Hello, is that a drop of rain?

CARLA: (*Holds out hand*) Moo, is that a drop of rain?

DILYS: (*Holds out hand*) Quack, is that a drop of rain?

ULYSSES: (*Holds out hand, strangulated noise*) Oh bum!

NARR: It rained for forty days and forty nights, and, as Noah had said, only the creatures aboard the ark survived the catastrophe. Carla the cow enjoyed her upper-deck cabin with sea views, and her species lived to tell the tale.

CARLA: Moo.

NARR: As did the descendants of Dilys the duck.

DILYS: Quack.

NARR: And as for Ulysses – well, to this day no one really knows what noise the unicorn made.

ULYSSES: (*Strangulated noise. Fade to blackout*)

BIBLE REFERENCE
Genesis chapters 6–8

Ulysses and Farquar

'We unicorns are the wisest species. We need no outside help – we just need to keep our wits about us'

INTRODUCTION

Over the years I've become quite attached to Ulysses from the previous sketch, so I decided to use him again, but this time in a more manageable two-hander. Here we meet him and his mate Farquar as they try to avoid Noah and his questionable animal-grabbing techniques!

Characters: ULYSSES; FARQUAR.

ULYSSES and FARQUAR both rush on stage, out of breath, and look for somewhere to hide.

ULYSSES: Check they're not coming round the back.

FARQUAR: All clear this way.

ULYSSES: Thank goodness. I think we'll be safe here for a bit.

FARQUAR: I'm absolutely shattered. I'm not cut out for all this dashing about.

ULYSSES: Well, it's better than the alternative, isn't it?

FARQUAR: You're not wrong there.

ULYSSES: I hear they caught the poor hedgehogs earlier.

FARQUAR: Oh no, poor things! What did they ever do to anyone?

ULYSSES: Well, I always found them a tad prickly – do you get it?

FARQUAR: Oh yes, very amusing.

ULYSSES: I thought so.

FARQUAR: By the time those guys have finished there'll be none of the animal kingdom left. We must be about the last ones.

ULYSSES: The word on the street is that a few species did make a dash up north.

FARQUAR: Oh yeah, who were they?

ULYSSES: Well, Derek the dodo was in charge, but he'd dragged along the hinglebots, the peladachs and the canglehumps.

FARQUAR: Perhaps we should have joined them.

ULYSSES: Rubbish! We unicorns are the wisest species. We need no outside help – just to keep our wits about us.

FARQUAR: That soppy old duffer and his big boat, does he realise how crazy he looks?

ULYSSES: It's not Noah I'm worried about, it's his psychotic sons and their questionable animal-grabbing techniques.

FARQUAR: They won't catch us, though, will they?

ULYSSES: Of course not! Shem, Ham and Japheth, huh! What a daft name Ham is!

FARQUAR: You can talk.

ULYSSES: And what's that supposed to mean?

FARQUAR: Well, 'Ulysses'!

ULYSSES: It's a very distinguished name, I'll have you know. It's also a lot better than Farquar!

FARQUAR: Okay, keep your voice down – we're supposed to be hiding.

ULYSSES: Good point. Let's check the perimeters again. (*They check*) All clear this end.

FARQUAR: Oh no!

ULYSSES: What is it?

FARQUAR: It's the giraffes! They've caught the giraffes!

ULYSSES: I suppose they held out well, considering how tricky it must be for them to hide. Are they on the ark?

FARQUAR: Sort of looks like they're on the top floor, with their heads sticking out the skylight.

ULYSSES: Oh, that really is the limit! Do they have no idea of health and safety?

FARQUAR: The whole ark is a total disaster.

ULYSSES: If it ever went on any water it would disintegrate in minutes.

FARQUAR: But of course it will never be on the water, because. . .

BOTH: . . .we're in the desert!

ULYSSES: Have you got any of those Doritos left?

FARQUAR: Yeah, hang on. . . Here you are.

ULYSSES: Any dip?

FARQUAR: Salsa, or onion and chive?

ULYSSES: Salsa.

(*Sound effect of closing of big door or distant thunder*)

FARQUAR: I should have warned you to take it easy with that salsa dip.

ULYSSES: That wasn't me!

FARQUAR: What was it, then?

ULYSSES: (*Checks*) Hello!

FARQUAR: What is it?

ULYSSES: The ark.

FARQUAR: Collapsed, has it?

ULYSSES: No, the door – it's closing!

FARQUAR: Closing? (*Sound effect of thunder*)

ULYSSES: Hello, what's this?

FARQUAR: Rain. It's called rain.

ULYSSES: Rain? Oh, I don't Adam-and-Eve it! (*Lights fade over sound effects of thunder and rain*)

BIBLE REFERENCE
Genesis chapter 7

Table Manners

'I'm a bit of a pro when it comes to hiding my true feelings, which was a shame on this occasion'

INTRODUCTION

The story of Gideon in Judges is one of my favourites in the Old Testament. How encouraging it is to read about God using this man to serve his purposes. I love the part where his already-out-numbered army of 32,000 gets whittled down to 300 – it's the stuff of legend, but just imagine the sheer horror if you had been one of the chosen 300! This piece takes us into the mind of one of those reluctant soldiers.

Character: NIGEL.

NIGEL: It's all my mother's fault – that's who I blame.

I know everyone always goes on about how their parents are the root of everything bad that's ever happened in their lives, 'cos they believe Freud and all those other philosophy and psychology types, but in my case it's true! You see, she always insisted we had these strict table manners, me and my other siblings. Elbows on the table, for a start, were a mortal sin as far as mother was concerned. They would only need to hover in the general direction of the table top and she would just about have a seizure. And when it comes to eating soup – well, any self-respecting person would surely allow a certain degree of slurping. It's only natural. Not my mother. Not even the slightest sip or slurp was to be audible. The whole process had to be conducted in absolute silence.

So you see, the whole polite manners thing has always been ingrained in me. Anyhow, I've leapt forward in my story to tell you all that, so let me put the thing in a bit of context for you.

I'm an Israelite by birth and, since finishing my education, have had a variety of jobs, including gas pump attendant and waiter at the Mount Gilead branch of Starbucks. Recently, though, I've joined up with around 32,000 foot soldiers under the command of Gideon, attempting to escape the oppression of the evil, occupying Midianites. Now 32,000 might sound a lot to wage war with, but with all their neighbouring allies the Midianites outnumber us somewhat. So when we were camped out by the spring of Harod there was a kind of low-key atmosphere. In actual fact, if the truth be known, a good number of our army were literally trembling with fear – not a few little jitters, you understand, or butterflies in the tummy, but the full-on wobbles, knees knocking, teeth chattering, the works! But not me! Not 'cos I'm brave, no way, but my polite upbringing had come with a stiff-upper-lip attitude. So I'm a bit of a pro when it comes to hiding my true feelings, which was a shame on this occasion. You see, Gideon had one of his 'words from the Lord'. He gets them all the time – a kind of bluetooth connection to the Almighty. Anyway, he decrees that anyone trembling with fear should go home.

Well, can you believe it? 'Mass exodus' would be a gross understatement – 22,000 of them went altogether, wobbling and shaking all the way home, a few of them faking it, in my opinion. And in one go our army is reduced to 10,000.

Still, I thought, 10,000 is a good number, enough to seriously kick some Midianite rear end.

Next thing, Gideon, bless him, gives us all permission before battle to wander down to the spring and enjoy some refreshing water. And this, in case you were wondering, is where my mother and her table manners come in. You see, in a situation like this, what would you do? You've a thirst on you like nobody's business, and in front of you is the most glorious, refreshing spring of cool, fresh water anywhere in the land. Well, you drop to your knees and stick your head in, don't you? Not me, though. No, I had visions of mother and the slurping soup – (*Imitates mother's voice*) 'Decorum, dear, decorum costs nothing!' So I squatted by the spring and delicately scooped water into my hand and lapped it up, with no noise whatsoever, I hasten to add.

What's wrong with that, you may ask – no problem there! And there wasn't. Not until Gideon had another one of his little 'words from the Lord'. This time, everyone who dropped to their knees and stuck their head in the water was sent home. Out of 10,000 that totalled 9,700. Just 300 of us left – 300! And although you might have thought it was at least the best 300 soldiers – you know, the ones who were most alert to what was going on around them – I'm afraid you'd be wrong. Take Arnold Grubble for a start. Best soldier we had, could knock the block off a dozen Midianites with a single swing of his club – but he's been sent home for shoving his head in the spring! No, you're not left with the best soldiers, only the most polite ones!

So, here we are, just the 300 of us now, preparing for battle with our illustrious leader, Gideon. He seems pretty upbeat, considering the earth-shatteringly depressing odds of survival. He's charging around the camp giving his orders. 'Watch me, follow my lead – for the Lord and for Gideon!' It's amazing, really, 'cos not so long ago he was famous for being the puniest member of possibly the wussiest family in our whole region. Still, times change, I suppose. And very shortly, with a blow of the trumpets, and after some slightly odd jar-smashing ritual, all 300 of us will charge into our suicide mission with aplomb.

And your role in this – the reason I'm telling you all this, when I'm normally an extremely private person – is a very simple one. If I don't make it back, and this death-charge leads to total destruction, I wonder if you could convey a message to my mother. Tell her that I never shirked from my responsibility, not once. I never took the easy way out and came home, though there was plenty of opportunity. But most importantly, and don't forget this, tell her that to the end, on the banks of the spring, my table manners remained impeccable. That'll mean so much to her.

'Watch me, follow me! For the Lord and for Gideon!'

Don't forget now, will you?

BIBLE REFERENCE
Judges chapter 7

Jerry and Ko

'I could feel a bit of the stonework crumbling away from my nether regions. It's been giving me right jip ever since!'

INTRODUCTION

It's always quite good fun to imagine familiar stories from the Bible and look at them from a slightly different perspective. In this sketch we look at the story of the walls of Jericho tumbling down, but from the bird's-eye view of the two main pillars on the gates of the wall. How might they have reported the rather strange proceedings?

Characters: JERRY; KO.

KO: Morning, Jerry.

JERRY: Morning, Ko.

KO: Good night's rest?

JERRY: Oh, you know, average, I suppose. You?

KO: Bit restless, to be honest, Jerry.

JERRY: Oh yeah, what was the problem?

KO: Well, I could feel a bit of the stonework crumbling off my nether regions. It's been giving me right jip ever since!

JERRY: Sorry to hear that, Ko. Still, there it is, being the pillar of a city is no easy task.

KO: You're not wrong there. People think it's easy just standing here looking imposing.

JERRY: Well, standing still is no easy task in itself, is it? You try to name any other creature in God's creation that could do it. No, the whole lot of them fidget around like they have swarms of ants in their pants.

KO: Proud of my role, though, Jerry.

JERRY: Me too, Ko. Making sure Jericho is shut tight. No one gets in that shouldn't, no one gets out that shouldn't. And that is down to you and me.

KO: 'Tis boring, though.

JERRY: Tell me about it.

KO: For instance, how many times have we had this self-same conversation?

JERRY: Ooh, I dunno, must be in the thousands.

KO: Well, we must have been stood here a good few years.

JERRY: A good few years? It's in the centuries, Ko, and no sign of retirement either. I could do with an easy gig. Lying down all day as a low wall in a field in Surrey would do me a treat.

KO: Oh, don't get me started! Wishful thinking, eh? Oh, I'm so bored!

JERRY: Fancy playing a game?

KO: Go on, then, what do you fancy?

JERRY: I spy with my little eye?

KO: Not again.

JERRY: Something beginning with M.

KO: Mountains?

JERRY: First time, well done. Your turn.

KO: I spy with my little eye something beginning with G.

JERRY: Ooh, tricky one. Is it grass?

KO: Yep! Well, that's that game finished, then.

JERRY: Have you seen our friends again today?

KO: Oh yeah, they must be shattered. How many days have they been hiking around the city walls?

JERRY: Six. Today will be the seventh.

KO: And they're still at it.

JERRY: You'll never guess how many times they've walked

around already today. I was watching before you woke up.

KO: What, more than once?

JERRY: Yeah, go on – have a guess.

KO: Oh, I dunno, three?

JERRY: Higher.

KO: Four?

JERRY: No, keep going up.

KO: Come on, just tell me.

JERRY: Okay, moody! It's six. This is their seventh now.

KO: Seven times! I wonder what it's all in aid of.

JERRY: Well, the one with the big beard is in charge. His name is Joshua. And he reckons – you won't believe this – that when they finish the seventh circuit, those guys will blow their horns and the city walls will crumble.

KO: Have you been drinking again?

JERRY: No, straight up! You just wait – when they finish this circuit, they'll blow them horns, guaranteed.

KO: Oh, I've got to see this. I mean, what a sauce! As if tooting some naff horn is going to cause us to come tumbling down. Think what we've withstood over the years.

JERRY: Look, here they come, the blokes with their horns.

KO: Ooh, I'm quaking in my boots, Jerry. Just wait for the deafening noise!

(*Sound effects of horns being sounded, ending with a long blast*)

KO: Is that it? Well, they've got to be gutted, hiking around for the last week and that's it! What an anticlimax.

(*Sound effects of distant shouting*)

JERRY: What are they shouting about?

KO: Well, if you'd wasted a week on some futile mission you'd have something to shout about, too!

JERRY: Fair point.

KO: Still, at least it relieved the boredom for a bit, eh?

JERRY: (*Pause*) Fancy another game, then?

KO: No, I've had enough excitement for one day, thanks.

JERRY: (*Pause*) Ko?

KO: Yes, Jerry.

JERRY: I might be displaying a rare moment of paranoia, but I'm feeling a bit shaky on my legs.

KO: Funny you should say that Jerry, my knees are feeling a bit – well, a bit jelly-like.

JERRY: Do you think it's got anything to do with – well, you know what?

KO: No! Well, maybe – but whoever is going to believe it? Just ask yourself that. (*Lights fade over sound effects of the crumbling of the city walls*)

BIBLE REFERENCE

Joshua chapter 5

Hiding the Forbidden Fruit

'What was all that about, hiding an apple core from the Lord of all creation behind your back?'

INTRODUCTION

I've always enjoyed the account of God confronting Adam and Eve with their sin in the Garden of Eden: they display their humanity in their efforts of concealment of their wrongdoing, and in their last-ditch attempts to pass the blame on. Although the piece is intended to be comedic, at the end it should make a powerful point about the consequence of sin.

Characters: ADAM; EVE; GOD (offstage voice only).

ADAM is alone onstage. There is an apple core on the ground.

GOD: Adam?

ADAM: Agghh! Oh, hello, God.

GOD: Are you okay, Adam?

ADAM: Yes, God, fine, God, everything's absolutely tickety-boo, God.

GOD: (*Doubtful*) Adam?

ADAM: What?

GOD: What have you been up to?

ADAM: Nothing.

GOD: Are you sure?

ADAM: Honestly.

GOD: Why are you covering yourself up, then?

ADAM: Er, good question. Well, I thought with you being the

Lord of all creation it was a bit disrespectful to go around in the nude.

GOD: It never bothered you before.

ADAM: Fair point, but between you and me it gets very draughty, and it's embarrassing.

GOD: Embarrassing?

ADAM: Yeah, just a bit, what with Eve being around.

GOD: Have you been eating fruit from the tree of knowledge?

ADAM: Me, God? No, God! Of course not, God.

GOD: Where did that apple core come from, then?

ADAM: (*Sees apple core and steps on it*) What apple core is that, then?

GOD: The one under your foot.

ADAM: (*Lifts other foot*) Nothing there, God.

GOD: The other one.

ADAM: (*Lifts foot and feigns shock*) Oh! Ah, that one.

GOD: Yes, Adam, that one.

ADAM: Er, well, yes – you see, that belongs to Eve.

GOD: What did you say?

ADAM: (*Louder*) It belongs to Eve.

EVE: (*Offstage*) Did you call me?

ADAM: Agghh! Yes – no – I –

EVE: Oh, make your mind up. Look, are you decent yet? If I have to see you walking around starkers any more I'll go and throw my apple up all over the place.

ADAM: Sshh!

EVE: Don't sshh me!

ADAM: Well, keep quiet then – we've got a guest.

EVE: Who? If it's that serpent again you can tell him to get lost.

ADAM: No, it's not the serpent.

EVE: Who is it, then? This is supposed to be a garden of tranquillity. (*EVE enters, eating an apple and smoking*)

GOD: Hello, Eve.

EVE: (*Spits out apple, stamps on cigarette and hides apple behind back*) Ooh, hello, God! What a lovely surprise!

GOD: What have you got there?

EVE: (*Indicating ADAM*) That? It's just a big cowardy-cowardy custard – you get used to him after a while.

GOD: No, not Adam! I mean what's in your hand?

EVE: (*Holds out hand*) Nothing.

GOD: Here we go again! The other one.

EVE: (*Switches apple and holds out other hand*) Nothing there either.

GOD: Both together.

EVE: (*Reluctantly brings out both hands*) Ooh, where did that come from?

GOD: I would hazard a guess from the tree of knowledge.

EVE: Ah, you know. . . Well, strictly speaking, it wasn't my fault. It was that serpent, slithering around and offering us all sorts.

GOD: Don't you worry about the serpent, I have a punishment ready for him, but that doesn't let you two off the hook.

ADAM: But it wasn't my fault – she made me do it!

EVE: Ooh, you spineless fibber!

ADAM: I am not spineless.

EVE: Yes you are.

ADAM: Am not.

EVE: Are too.

ADAM: Am not.

EVE: Are too.

GOD: (*Interrupts but ADAM and EVE continue bickering*) Children! (*Louder*) Children! (*They stop*) Look at me! You were my first two children, whom I adored above all creation. For you I made this idyllic garden, and I delighted to see you enjoy it. I wanted to give you immortal life in this paradise of Eden. But you disobeyed me, and, worse still, you tried to hide that disobedience from me, as if that were possible. Your punishment, then, is expulsion from the Garden of Eden. Never again will you return to this paradise.

ADAM: Oh, but God –

EVE: He's gone.

ADAM: Well, this is a right pickle you've got us into!

EVE: Me?

ADAM: Yes, you! I told you that serpent was a bit iffy.

EVE: Oh, that's easy to say now.

ADAM: And what was all that about, hiding an apple from the Lord of all creation behind your back? (*Mimics her*) 'Ooh, where did that come from?' Pathetic!

EVE: You can talk. (*Mimics*) 'It wasn't my fault – she made me do it!' Typical man!

ADAM: What do you mean, 'typical man'? I'm the only man!

EVE: Exactly! (*Pause*) Look, let's stop arguing, eh? It's just about doing my head in.

ADAM: (*Pause*) I'm really going to miss this place.

EVE: Yeah, me too. Come on, let's pack – and leave that apple behind!

BIBLE REFERENCE
Genesis 3

Restless Night

'The boy must have problems with his ears. Have you had him checked for tinnitus?'

Characters: ELI; MICHAEL.

ELI and MICHAEL are both dozing on chairs. ELI suddenly wakes up.

ELI: Oh no, not again! Michael? Michael!

MICHAEL: (*Jumps*) Who goes there? I'm armed and dangerous, I warn you!

ELI: Don't panic – it's only me, Michael.

MICHAEL: What are you doing making me jump out of my skin?

ELI: Nothing. It's just that we've done it again.

MICHAEL: Eh? Oh, not again!

ELI: How many days straight is that?

MICHAEL: Oh, twelve, maybe thirteen.

ELI: Must be a record. Still, I have got an excuse, at least.

MICHAEL: Who needs an excuse? Two old men sharing a few drinks and boring conversation – of course we're going to drop off.

ELI: It's so embarrassing, though. As a kid I remember watching my dad fall asleep at the drop of a hat. As soon as he sat down, he would be snoring like a pig. I swore I would never be the same.

MICHAEL: Enjoy it, Eli. It comes to us all – the privilege of old age. Anyway, what was this excuse?

ELI: Excuse?

MICHAEL: You just said you had a good excuse for dropping off.

ELI: Oh yes, so I did.

MICHAEL: Not been out on the town, have you? Inappropriate for someone in your position.

ELI: Of course not! No, last night I had a rather restless night.

MICHAEL: You should try Gaviscon. Tastes revolting but settles you down a treat.

ELI: It's nothing to do with my stomach – it was the boy.

MICHAEL: Oh, he's got to that age, has he? Drunken parties, late nights and devilish young ladies.

ELI: No, Michael. Your mind is always in the gutter.

MICHAEL: I'm just being a realist.

ELI: You don't know this boy.

MICHAEL: Come on, then, enlighten me.

ELI: Well, last night, it was after one o'clock, I was fast asleep dreaming of happier times – my sons away, travelling, experiencing the world – when all of a sudden I was woken. And standing at the foot of my bed was a shadowy figure.

MICHAEL: Not robbers? Oh, this city is becoming intolerable.

ELI: No, not robbers – it was young Samuel. Standing there in his pyjamas and night cap. 'You called me, master,' he says. 'What do you want?'

MICHAEL: Why did you call the boy at one in the morning?

ELI: I hadn't – that's what I'm saying. I told him he was dreaming and sent him back to bed. Off he went, and I went back to sleep, thinking nothing of it.

MICHAEL: Well, as stories go, Eli, this one isn't that riveting!

ELI: I'm not finished yet. It can't have been a quarter of an hour later when I was woken again, this time by the distinct aroma of Marmite.

MICHAEL: Marmite? Yuk! Whoever created that stuff should be shot.

ELI: Couldn't agree more – revolting stuff.

MICHAEL: So where was the smell coming from?

ELI: Young Samuel again. He always has a slice of toast with Marmite before he goes to bed. And as I opened my eyes, there he was again, kneeling on my bed and whispering in my ear, 'Here I am, master. You called me.'

MICHAEL: The boy must have problems with his ears. Have you had him checked for tinnitus?

ELI: It has nothing to do with tinnitus! Anyway, that's ringing in your ears – this is mysterious voices.

MICHAEL: Okay, Doctor Eli, so what happened next?

ELI: Well, I was somewhat irked, to be honest. I sent him back to bed and told him in no uncertain terms to get back to sleep.

MICHAEL: Well, the boy can't help dreaming. Maybe it's the effect of the Marmite.

ELI: It was no such thing – he's been eating it since forever.

MICHAEL: So did you get to sleep after that?

ELI: No, hardly another wink all night. It happened again, you see. He wanders in, all wide-eyed and innocent. 'Here I am, master. You called.' And that's when it struck me, what I'd known deep down all along.

MICHAEL: What, that Samuel's a bit of a nutcase?

ELI: No! That he wasn't hearing things – that he was hearing God.

MICHAEL: You think so.

ELI: I know so.

MICHAEL: So what did you do?

ELI: Sent him back to his room. I told him to lie down and, if he heard that voice again, to say, 'Speak, Lord, for your servant is listening.'

MICHAEL: And did it work?

ELI: Oh yes, it worked – it worked.

MICHAEL: What did he say?

ELI: Many things – wonderful but terrible things.

MICHAEL: Then he's a prophet, Eli! Young Samuel is a prophet.

ELI: Yeah. (*Distracted*) 'Master, you called me. . . here I am. . . here I am. . .'

BIBLE REFERENCE

1 Samuel 3

Konichiwa!

'This is utterly ridiculous! We can't spend the rest of our lives spouting random tripe like that!'

INTRODUCTION

Ever since my school days I have come humbly to accept that when it comes to speaking foreign languages, I am seriously pants! At exams I was a complete failure, and in my adult travels I have fared little better, often making a complete idiot of myself in social situations. As the Tower of Babel was erected and society became confident in its ability to succeed, what a shocker it must have been to wake up one morning and realise the basic ability to communicate had disappeared.

Characters: MAN; WOMAN.

MAN:	You back already, love?
WOMAN:	(*Offstage and flustered*) Yes, I am.
MAN:	Get what you needed?
WOMAN:	Ha!
MAN:	Oh blimey!
WOMAN:	(*Enters*) Funny you should ask, but no, I did not get what I want.
MAN:	What's the problem, love?
WOMAN:	I'll tell you what the problem is, Jeremy – the world has gone totally mad. Utterly, utterly bonkers!
MAN:	Is that all? I could have told you that before you went out.

WOMAN: Oh no. You couldn't have told me this. Wait until you hear what I've had to put up with this morning.

MAN: I'm all ears, my love.

WOMAN: Okay, so I pop in to see Priscilla in the linen store to give her the measurements for my new curtains.

MAN: *Our* new curtains!

WOMAN: Oh, don't interrupt, Jeremy! You can be so infuriating.

MAN: Sorry, carry on.

WOMAN: I went in to see Priscilla about our new curtains, expecting to be greeted in her usual polite and professional manner, but you'll never guess what she said to me. Well, go on then, have a guess!

MAN: Oh, I don't know – was it rude?

WOMAN: I haven't the faintest idea.

MAN: You don't know if it was rude? What are you going on about?

WOMAN: I can hardly bring myself to utter what she said.

MAN: Well, come on, force yourself! I haven't got all day.

WOMAN: She said – konichiwa.

MAN: Konichi what?

WOMAN: Koinchiwa! I know – shocking, isn't it?

MAN: What does it mean?

WOMAN: How should I know? Does it look like I speak foreign?

MAN: So why was Priscilla from the linen shop talking foreign?

WOMAN: Well, the word on the street is that something funny's happened with everyone's speech.

MAN: Something funny? What, funny ha-ha or funny peculiar?

WOMAN: Funny peculiar, you great berk! There's people you used to converse with, no problem, and all of a sudden you can't make head or tail of a word they say.

MAN: What language is it, then?

WOMAN: Oh, a bit of everything – Dutch, Swedish, Chinese,

Urdu. Apparently Daphne from the greengrocer's is fluent in Swahili.

MAN: So how are we supposed to communicate?

WOMAN: Well, I popped into Jacob's bookstore on the way home to see if he could help.

MAN: And what did he have to say?

WOMAN: Funny you should ask that. I think it was something like, 'Ah, bonjour, Madame, qu'est-ce que je peux faire pour vous?'

MAN: Oh no! Him as well, then!

WOMAN: 'Fraid so. Still, I picked up a few foreign phrase books. They might come in useful.

MAN: Good idea. Are they any good?

WOMAN: Well, they're a bit random, to be honest.

MAN: Give us a preview, then.

WOMAN: Okay. 'Gai I wyboddeth am y milfeddygfa lleol os gwelwch chi'n dda?'

MAN: What's that, then?

WOMAN: It means, 'Can you give me directions to the nearest vet's?' in Welsh.

MAN: Oh, very useful. Anything else?

WOMAN: How about this one – 'tenen el voric?'

MAN: No idea.

WOMAN: That one's 'Do you like red sausage?' in Spanish.

MAN: This is utterly ridiculous! We can't spend the rest of our lives spouting random tripe like that.

WOMAN: Don't lose your rag with me! I told you the world's gone utterly bonkers!

MAN: I wonder what's caused it?

WOMAN: I don't know. Maybe it'll all clear up in a day or so and we can all get back to normal.

MAN: Let's hope so.

WOMAN: Ooh, I'm parched. I'm sticking the kettle on – fancy anything?

MAN: Si, caffe con lecce por vavour.

WOMAN: I beg your pardon?

MAN: Mmm? No l'entenc.

WOMAN: Oh, not you now! Tea? Coffee? *Coffee*?

MAN: Ah si, si, caffe con lecce.

WOMAN: Coffee and letchy? What's he on about?

MAN: (*Slowly, while miming 'cup' and 'milking'*) Caffe – con lecce – lecce – (*Mimics cow*) Moo!

WOMAN: Ah oui, oui, café au lait, monsieur.

MAN: Eh?

WOMAN: Je voudrais un café au lait. Ooh la-la! Magnifique! C'est magnifique! (*Lights fade to blackout*)

BIBLE REFERENCE
Genesis 11:1–9

Delicate Touch

'Well, to cut a long story short, I need to cut his hair'

INTRODUCTION

Well, it's all very well finding out you need to cut Samson's hair to make him lose his strength. But if you have no skills in barbering, what are you to do? Here we find the ever-so-cunning Delilah taking a few tips from her hair stylist, Stacy.

Characters: DELILAH; STACY.

DELILAH is seated, reading a newspaper. STACY dashes in.

STACY: Hello, sugar plum, sorry to keep you waiting.

DELILAH: No problem, Stacy.

STACY: You are looking totally gorgeous as ever – who's your hair stylist and beautician?

DELILAH: Well, I don't know, but she must be the best in the business!

STACY: Oh, stop it, you're too kind! Now let's be having a look at you. (*Inspects DELILAH's hair*) Roots are looking lovely, basic shape is holding up – very good. Are you using that conditioner with essence of jojoba I recommended?

DELILAH: Of course.

STACY: Every day?

DELILAH: Well, maybe not quite every day.

STACY: Naughty girl! You must do what the doctor tells you. Now promise me, essence of jojoba every day!

DELILAH: Okay, Stacy, I promise.

STACY: Good girl.

DELILAH: Business going well, is it?

STACY: Oh yeah, rushed off my feet, I am. Took another stylist on a few weeks back.

DELILAH: Any good?

STACY: Well, as good as can be expected. Not up to my standards, you understand.

DELILAH: Well, of course.

STACY: She hasn't got my delicate touch. Mind you, that can't be taught – you've either got it or you haven't.

DELILAH: No, I agree. And how's the love-life?

STACY: Ooh, my current one is a Philistine.

DELILAH: Oh dear – lacking on the cultural front?

STACY: No! He literally is a Philistine – one of their soldiers. Strapping lad, he is, but I can't see it lasting long. You still with your Samson?

DELILAH: Mmm, sort of. . .

STACY: That doesn't sound too healthy! I thought you two were set up till death us do part.

DELILAH: Well, in a manner of speaking that could be true.

STACY: Hello, Delilah, this sounds intriguing!

DELILAH: Look, can I trust you to keep a secret?

STACY: Come on now, Delilah! You know my opinion on this – the relationship between hair stylist and client is one of total confidentiality, a little bit like the confessional.

DELILAH: Of course. Well, to be honest I'm getting a bit fed up with Samson. He's so impetuous, and the Philistines have offered to make it worth my while to hand him over.

STACY: Yeah well, my current conquest has mentioned something about this. Keeps going wrong, though – your Samson is too strong for them all.

DELILAH: True, the plan has had its teething problems, but at last I think I have the secret.

STACY: Ooh, I love a secret! Go on.

DELILAH: Well, I know how to weaken him, 100 per cent guaranteed. But I need your help.

STACY: Mine? How can I help?

DELILAH: Well, to cut a long story short, I need to cut his hair short.

STACY: Cut his hair?

DELILAH: Sshh! His strength is in his long Nazirite hair – cut it off and he'll be putty in the Philistine's hands.

STACY: So what you want off me is hairdressing tips.

DELILAH: Exactly. It's got to be shaved, but I need to do it with your famous delicate touch, Stace, or he'll wake up and suss what's going on.

STACY: Well, I can certainly give you some advice there, love. I've got a lovely set of Nicky Clarke clippers out back you can borrow. He won't feel a thing.

DELILAH: You're a star. It's good to have someone to confide in.

STACY: That's what I'm here for, sweetheart. When are you planning on doing it?

DELILAH: Tonight – it's all set up with the army.

STACY: Blimey, that quick? I don't mean to cast doubts, love, but what are they planning to do with Samson once they've captured him?

DELILAH: I don't know – not really thought about that.

STACY: It's just that they are Philistines, remember – not exactly famous for their delicate touch, if you know what I mean.

DELILAH: I see your point. Do you think I'm making a mistake?

STACY: No comment, pet, no comment. I give advice on perms, not moral dilemmas.

DELILAH: Haven't really thought much beyond the reward – my chance to get rich, really rich!

STACY: Well, you'd better still get your hair done here after you get all high and mighty.

DELILAH: Of course I will, you know that.

STACY: I'll get you them clippers, then – if you're really sure?

DELILAH: Yeah, I'm sure. (*STACY exits*) I think I'm sure. . .

BIBLE REFERENCE

Judges chapter 16

New Testament

Clear Vision

'Not that pool of Siloam! I've told you not to go there – it's filthy!'

INTRODUCTION

Jesus's miracles must have had a huge impact on many people, and these transformations are often illustrated in the Gospel accounts. But not everyone's reaction is explained. This sketch looks at the story of the boy who was given back his sight. How would his parents have reacted to this event?

Characters: MAN; WOMAN; BOY.

WOMAN: Where is he? I said, where is he?

MAN: Eh?

WOMAN: *Where is he?*

MAN: Who? What are you on about?

WOMAN: Who, he says, who! Who do you think, David Beckham?

MAN: David Beckham? I'm not with you, love.

WOMAN: Your son, you daft ha'p'orth! Where's our flipping son?

MAN: Oh well, on his way, I suppose.

WOMAN: On his way? It's half past six!

MAN: And?

WOMAN: And? You know my tummy starts making all sorts of funny noises if I eat after six.

MAN: Well, go and have a chocolate hobnob or something, then! Creeping ivy!

WOMAN: I don't know why I bother. For all the thanks I get I

might as well knock you up spaghetti hoops on toast
every night and be done with it. My chicken cordon
bleu is congealing by the second out there.

MAN: Calm down.

WOMAN: You just don't care, do you? He's probably lost his
cane. You know he can't go anywhere without his
cane. Oh, he'll be crashing into things left, right and
centre. He'll come back all bloody and bruised – if he
makes it back at all, that is. (*She cries hysterically*)

(*BOY enters*)

BOY: I'm back.

WOMAN: Where have you been? I've been worried sick.

BOY: Just out.

WOMAN: Where?

BOY: Somewhere.

WOMAN: Oh, I give up! And where's your cane?

BOY: Leave me alone!

WOMAN: I told you, didn't I? I said I bet he's lost his cane.

MAN: Well, he's home now, so let's all calm down.

WOMAN: *I am calm!* I am the epitome of calmness.

MAN: You been down by the pool with your mates?

BOY: Yeah.

WOMAN: Not that pool of Siloam! I've told you not to go there
– it's filthy!

BOY: Well, I like it there. It's cool.

WOMAN: It's not cool, it's infested. And I bet you left your cane
up there.

BOY: Yeah, not bothered though, don't even want it.

WOMAN: Don't be so silly. How are you gonna find your way
around without your cane?

BOY: Found my way home, didn't I?

WOMAN: Well, anyone can find their way home, but how are
you going to find anywhere else?

BOY: With my eyes.

WOMAN: I can't talk to him any more.

MAN: Come on, son, you know you're blind.

BOY: Not any more. As of this afternoon I can see perfectly.

WOMAN: Oh, he's having one of his delusions again.

BOY: *I'm not!*

MAN: So what are you trying to say, exactly?

BOY: I was blind but now I can see. Test me if you don't believe me.

MAN: All right! How many fingers am I holding up? (*MAN holds up fingers and boy responds correctly*)

BOY: 5. . . 4. . . 3. . .

WOMAN: Okay, we get the point. Let's have a look at these eyes, then. Oh, look at the state of them! You've got patches of mud all over you. (*WOMAN spits on tissue and starts to clean BOY's face*)

BOY: Mum!

WOMAN: Well, how did you manage that?

BOY: It was the man they call Jesus. He made some mud and put it on my eyes. Then he told me to wash in the pool of Siloam, and I did and then I could see.

WOMAN: Mud on your eyes? I told you that pool of Siloam was filthy dirty.

MAN: So you can really see? You're not winding us up?

BOY: No, I really can see.

MAN: It's amazing – our boy can see!

WOMAN: Where is this Jesus now?

BOY: I don't know.

MAN: Well, I'd like to find him. I'd like to thank him.

WOMAN: Oh no, don't get involved with him. I've heard about him down at the market, upsetting the Pharisees, and what with today being the Sabbath there'll be trouble.

MAN: We can't just forget this – it's a miracle! Our blind son can see!

WOMAN: But what will the authorities say about it? Think of our standing in the community. I'm up for chairperson of the local WI.

BOY: I'll just tell them what I know. I don't know who this bloke is, but I was blind and now I can see – end of.

WOMAN: But they're all saying he's a sinner. A blasphemer!

BOY: Mum, a sinner can't open the eyes of a blind man. If he's not from God, he couldn't do a thing.

MAN: I think he's right, love. I fear he's right.

WOMAN: But what will we say to the Pharisees?

MAN: I don't know. (*MAN and WOMAN turn to BOY*)

BOY: (*Pause*) Well, don't look at me!

BIBLE REFERENCE
John 9: 1–38

Chariot Boot Sale

'Utterly genius. Roll up on your chariot, flip up the boot and get rid of all your junk – marvellous!'

INTRODUCTION

Even with John the Baptist telling people to prepare the way of the Lord, many misunderstood and saw him (John) as the Messiah. This could of course prove problematic if you'd made an unwise investment in that belief!

Characters: ONE; TWO.

ONE and TWO stand behind tables loaded with goods.

ONE: Well, there's a right load of tripe for sale here, isn't there?

TWO: What's that, mate?

ONE: All these stalls. Selling a right load of tripe.

TWO: Yeah, you noticed.

ONE: It beggars belief that people actually buy it.

TWO: Well, humans are daft, aren't they? Buy anything if they think it's a bargain.

ONE: Good idea, though, these chariot boot sales.

TWO: Genius. Utterly genius. Roll up on your chariot, flip up the boot and get rid of all your junk – marvellous!

ONE: See that bloke over there?

TWO: Which one?

ONE: Him there – long straggly black beard and a dodgy comb-over.

TWO: Oh yeah.

ONE: He's trying to flog his old pair of sandals. I mean, I ask you!

TWO: Unbelievable, isn't it?

ONE: The soles on them are so worn you can see daylight straight through them.

TWO: But I guarantee that by the end of the day some dilly will have taken them off his hands.

ONE: Unbelievable!

TWO: Still, who are we to complain, eh? As long as I can shift some of my old tat, good luck to him and his scruffy sandals.

ONE: Hear-hear to that! What you got up for grabs, then?

TWO: Oh, a bit of everything. Loads of kids' clothes – been used by all our six, so they're wearing a bit thin.

ONE: Not holding on to them in case of a seventh?

TWO: No chance there – snippety-snip, if you catch my drift!

ONE: Oh, I see.

TWO: Got a few Mantovani tapes, a nice little selection of trinkets and ornaments. . . Basically, anything the missus has been hoarding for the past twenty years – all now for sale at a knock-down price. (*Calls out to passers-by*) Come on, ladies and gents, roll up, roll up, everything must go! (*To ONE*) What about you?

ONE: Just got the one item.

TWO: Blimey!

ONE: Well, I say one item – I've got stuck with a couple of thousand of that one item.

TWO: Oh, dearie dear! Let's have a look, then.

ONE: Well, me and my business partner had these printed up. (*Holds up a shirt with 'John the Baptist' printed on it*)

TWO: (*Reads*) 'John the Baptist.' Well, he's a popular man. Strange you can't shift them.

ONE: Ah, well, they're double-sided – check out the back.

(*Turns shirt round; the back reads 'is the Messiah'*)

TWO: (*Reads*) 'Is the Messiah.' Oh dear. I see your problem. Why did you have them done?

ONE: Well, at the time we thought he was. Everyone was excited about him going around in his camel's hair gear and baptising people. We thought, let's get ahead of the game and do some official merchandise.

TWO: Then the other one turns up.

ONE: Precisely. All of a sudden it's 'Prepare the way of the Lord.' 'Don't look at me, look at this Jesus fella.'

TWO: Good news about the true Messiah, though.

ONE: (*Ironically*) Oh yeah, fabulous. Totally wonderful. Now I'm stuck with two thousand shirts which are about as useful as a chocolate saucepan.

TWO: Have you tried to doctor them?

ONE: Eh?

TWO: You know, change the words around a bit.

ONE: Well, we did think about changing it to 'John the Baptist isn't the Messiah', but it's not overly catchy, is it?

TWO: No, fair point. Bit of a problem, then.

ONE: Just a bit. So here I am, trying to knock them out on the cheap. We're hoping to appeal to the young, ironic, postmodern type. You know, if you *believe* that John is the Messiah, then he is – know what I mean?

TWO: Not really, no. How many you sold?

ONE: None.

TWO: Oh dear.

ONE: Yeah, tell me about it.

TWO: How much you charging?

ONE: Half a denarius a piece. Less than cost, that is.

TWO: (*Pause*) Go on then, give us one!

ONE: Really?

TWO: Yeah, I've always fancied myself as a bit of a postmodernist.

ONE: Well, thank you for your custom, sir.

TWO: 'Tis a pleasure. Only one thousand nine hundred and ninety-nine to get shot of now – you're on a roll!

ONE: Yeah, no problem.

TWO: Want a helping hand?

ONE: Yeah!

BOTH: Come on, ladies and gents, bargain prices, everything must go!

BIBLE REFERENCE
Matthew chapter 3

The Miraculous Fall

'Dozed off? I thought you said his preaching was amazing. Sounds to me like it was pretty dull'

INTRODUCTION

Have you ever wondered what happened to that poor bloke that fell out of the window while Paul was preaching in the upper room? Me too! Read on to discover his quirky and original tale!

Characters: EUTYCHUS; TICHIUS.

EUTYCHUS is sitting up in a hospital bed reading. TICHIUS is waking from his slumber.

TICH: (*Groans*)

EUTY: You okay there, pal?

TICH: What's that?

EUTY: I said, are you okay? Sounds like you're in pain.

TICH: Oh, I'll be all right. It's always the same when I first wake up. I go into a kind of seizure.

EUTY: Anything I can do to help?

TICH: No, give me a couple of minutes and I'll be okay. (*Coughing fit*) Oh, for the love of saints!

EUTY: My name's Eutychus, by the way.

TICH: Oh, 'scuse my manners. I'm Tichius – pleasure to meet you.

EUTY: Been in here long, have you?

TICH: Oh, a couple of weeks, I think – I lose track. Still, nice break from the wife's cooking. They do us up a treat in here. Just in, yourself?

EUTY: Yeah, few hours ago.

TICH: What's up with you, then? You look as right as rain.

EUTY: Oh, just in for a check-up.

TICH: Sounds ominous. Serious, is it?

EUTY: No, not at all. I had a bit of a nasty fall, so my friends insisted I came in for a quick once-over.

TICH: Few too many sherbets, was it?

EUTY: Sorry?

TICH: A few too many sherbets, that preceded the fall?

EUTY: Oh, I see what you mean! No, nothing like that. Bit of a long story, if the truth be told.

TICH: Well, come on then, out with it! I haven't got anything better to do, have I?

EUTY: Well, have you heard of the preacher man they call Paul? Used to go by the name of Saul of Tarsus.

TICH: Saul. . . Wait a minute, isn't he the one who used to go around persecuting Christians?

EUTY: The very same. Anyway, I was with a group listening to Paul preach –

TICH: Any good, is he?

EUTY: Yeah, amazing – really amazing – and he was headed off the next day, so we were hanging on to his every word, making the most of him before he left.

TICH: This all happen local, did it?

EUTY: Yeah, in Troas. I was listening to him perched up on the window ledge.

TICH: On the window ledge? That's a daft place to sit, isn't it?

EUTY: Well, I don't make a habit of it, but the place was packed. It was the only spot I could find.

TICH: Oh, I see. Carry on, then.

EUTY: Thank you. So, it was getting late, all dark outside, lamps on in the room, and I started to – well, doze off.

TICH: Doze off? I thought you said his preaching was amazing? Sounds to me like it was pretty dull.

EUTY: No, not at all. I'd been up since the crack of dawn and, well, my eyes just couldn't stay open any longer.

TICH: So what happened then?

EUTY: I fell backwards out the window.

TICH: You what?

EUTY: I sank into a deep sleep, leant back and fell out the window.

TICH: Oh, my goodness, what a scene! Lucky for you it wasn't high up or it would have been more than a check-up you needed.

EUTY: In fact it was – three storeys up.

TICH: Three storeys? Don't be ridiculous! If you'd fallen down from that high up you'd have croaked instantly.

EUTY: I did!

TICH: (*Pause*) Sorry, I thought you said 'I did'.

EUTY: I did. I did croak, as you so delicately put it.

TICH: You see, I was following you perfectly until then, and now you've got me all confused.

EUTY: Well, as you can imagine my fall caused a bit of a stir. Everyone came rushing down to see me, and found me – well, dead.

TICH: I must say you're looking extremely healthy, considering.

EUTY: That's down to Paul. Apparently he came down, very distressed, threw himself on me, wrapped his arms around me and yelled out, 'He's alive!'

TICH: And you were?

EUTY: And I am!

TICH: And you're feeling okay?

EUTY: Better than ever. I'm only here to satisfy my overcautious friends.

TICH: And what about this Paul – is he coming to visit you?

EUTY: No, he's on his way to Assos now, spreading the message far and wide – the good news.

TICH: What good news is that, then?

EUTY: That death is defeated. That the Messiah has come.

TICH: And that miracles happen.

EUTY: Maybe that physical miracles point us to more important spiritual truths.

TICH: Good, very good. (*TICHIUS looks at menu card*) I've got some more good news for you.

EUTY: Oh, yeah, what's that?

TICH: Banana custard for dessert. They do a very good banana custard here.

EUTY: (*Half-heartedly*) Oh, good. . . I'll look forward to that. . .

BIBLE REFERENCE

Acts 20:7–12

The Wine Aficionado

'What are you on there – the cheeky little Pinot Grigio?'

INTRODUCTION

In the last few years it seems we have become a nation of wine fanatics. Not so long ago we would have been happy with a bottle of Blue Nun, but now the goal posts have moved rather. Here we can wonder what the guests at a certain wedding in Cana made of the wine.

Characters: ROGER; TERENCE; WAITER (walk-on).

ROGER: Hello there.

TERENCE: Hello.

ROGER: Wonderful party, isn't it?

TERENCE: Yes, terrific.

ROGER: Know how to organise a do, don't they?

TERENCE: Mmm?

ROGER: The Goldblatts. Really know how to put on a do.

TERENCE: Oh yes, they certainly do.

ROGER: Did you come to Angela's fortieth?

TERENCE: Er, no.

ROGER: Oh dear, you missed Angela's fortieth. Why was that?

TERENCE: Well, I wasn't invited.

ROGER: Oh, I'm terribly sorry, that was insensitive of me.

TERENCE: Don't worry. I wasn't expecting an invite. You see, I've absolutely no idea who Angela is.

ROGER: Don't know Angela? Angela Cynthia Goldblatt, mother of the bride.

TERENCE: Ah well, that explains it. I'm a friend of Henry's, the groom.

ROGER: Oh, how silly of me. Lovely chap, isn't he? Absolutely charming.

TERENCE: Well, you don't know him, of course.

ROGER: I'm sorry?

TERENCE: Nothing. He's an absolute charmer.

ROGER: Plonk's fantastic, isn't it?

TERENCE: Yes, it certainly was.

ROGER: What are you on there – the cheeky little Pinot Grigio?

TERENCE: No.

ROGER: The crisp Frascati?

TERENCE: No.

ROGER: Not the Pinot or Frascati? Looks a little clear for the Chardonnay. May I? (*Takes glass and smells the wine*) I'm getting melons, fresh summer apples and just a dash of macaroons.

TERENCE: (*Snatches back glass*) What you're getting is on my nerves!

ROGER: I'm sorry. Well, put me out of my misery – what is it?

TERENCE: It's the cheeky little Evian.

ROGER: Evian? Which grape is that from?

TERENCE: It's water, you berk, so I don't know where the dash of macaroons was from.

ROGER: Water? You're drinking water?

TERENCE: Yes! Is there a problem?

ROGER: Well, it's a bit sad, isn't it? This Cabernet is 14 per cent proof! I've had eight glasses and yet I'm not even slightly wasted.

TERENCE: Well, bully for you. I'm so impressed.

ROGER: Are you one of those weird teetotallers?

TERENCE: As a matter of fact, no. I happened to arrive a bit late, and thanks to certain people going a bit OTT, all the wine has gone.

ROGER: Rubbish! It's not all gone – there's gallons of the stuff.

TERENCE: Not when I got here half an hour ago.

ROGER: Ah, that was before the fella over there swung into action.

TERENCE: What are you babbling on about?

ROGER: Well, they did run out of wine for a bit – social faux pas of the decade – but, with a bit of prompting, up steps this bloke.

TERENCE: Who is he?

ROGER: Oh, I don't know – wasn't listening. From Nazareth or somewhere, I think. Anyway, he has a load of jugs filled with water, says abracadabra or hey presto, and out pops the juiciest little Cabernet this side of the Sea of Galilee.

TERENCE: Good story.

ROGER: More than a story – it's a fact.

TERENCE: Sure you've not overdosed there?

ROGER: No, I have not! I do know how to take my drink. Why don't you try a glass?

TERENCE: Go on, then.

ROGER: Good. (*Calls offstage*) Hey, you, bring us a glass of the new stuff! (*Waiter enters with glass on tray. TERENCE takes glass and waiter stands by*) Buzz off, then – yours is a non-speaking role. (*To TERENCE*) What do you think?

TERENCE: Pretty good.

ROGER: (*Sniffs*) I'm getting wild berries from the Amazon River, I'm getting cinnamon pine-cones, I'm getting the warming sun on my face on a summer's evening . . . You getting anything?

TERENCE: (*Burps*) Yeah, mate, I'm getting another glass.
             (*TERENCE exits*)
ROGER: (*Pause*) Drunkards!

BIBLE REFERENCE
John 2:1–11

The Destruction of Babylon

'I don't mean to spoil your fun, but Babylon's spelt with a Y!'

INTRODUCTION

In my first collection of sketches I introduced Walter, possibly the worst evangelist in the world. Here he returns to save the world from everlasting peril by predicting the destruction of Babylon – or is that Babilon?

Characters: WALTER; MAN; WOMAN (offstage only).

Dramatic music opens sketch. WALTER enters, holding a scythe. He knocks on a door.

MAN: I'll get it, love. (*Opens door*) Good grief! Who are you?

WOMAN: Who is it, love?

MAN: I dunno, love – the Grim Reaper, I think!

WALTER: I am not the Grim Reaper, but I bear grim news.

MAN: Oh no! (*To wife*) Did you renew the TV licence, love?

WOMAN: Yeah, course I did.

MAN: Oh, thank goodness for that. What's your problem, then, pal?

WALTER: I have no problem, but I am afraid you are in great danger.

MAN: If it's double-glazing you're selling, we're fully done.

WALTER: The end is nigh, hear ye all – *the end is nigh!*

MAN: Pipe down, man! The missus is watching *EastEnders* in there. If you disturb her, she'll come out here and make *your* end nigh.

WALTER: Do not spurn me, sir. Do not reject me. It will be at your peril. I bring a grave warning, to shake you into sacrificial repentance and flagellation before the Almighty.

MAN: Ooh, that doesn't sound very comfy.

WALTER: Believe me, it's nothing in comparison with the torments of the fiery depths of hell.

MAN: Oh, I see. . . Have you escaped from somewhere?

WALTER: *Yes!* I have escaped from my enslavement to sinful desires! I have been released and am preparing to return home.

MAN: Well, is there someone I can telephone for you?

WALTER: (*Shaking scythe*) Where I'm going has no telephones, you foolish plebeian!

MAN: Be careful there, you'll have someone's eye out with that scythe!

WOMAN: Roger, are you coming back in?

MAN: Yes, just a moment, I'm discussing the fiery depths of hell.

WOMAN: Oh, it's not those Jehovah's Witnesses again?

MAN: No – well, maybe, I don't know. Who are you exactly?

WALTER: That's what I've been trying to tell you. My name is Walter, and I'm here to warn you of the impending destruction of Babylon.

MAN: Oh, well, ta for the warning.

WALTER: Prophecies will be fulfilled, tongues will cease and the final seal will be opened. Armageddon is at hand.

MAN: And when's all this supposed to happen?

WALTER: A week next Tuesday.

MAN: That soon? Very specific date you have there.

WALTER: Ah, it's a very careful mathematical calculation based on codes hidden in the pages of Scripture.

MAN: Have you been reading that *Da Vinci Code*?

WALTER: No! Utter tripe. By assigning to each of the letters of the word 'Babylon' a numerical value, and applying a carefully constructed equation, the date is clearly evident. Armageddon is a week next Tuesday.

MAN: How did you work it out?

WALTER: You take the letters (*Spells them out*) B A B I L O N.

MAN: Come again?

WALTER: B A B I –

MAN: Slight problem, Walter.

WALTER: What's that?

MAN: Well, I don't mean to spoil your fun, but 'Babylon' is spelt with a Y.

WALTER: Eh?

MAN: (*Spells letters*) B A B Y L O N.

WALTER: Oh, I see. . .

MAN: Maybe you should recalculate.

WALTER: Yes, well, that's simple enough. (*Fiddles with calculator*) Aha! The destruction of Babylon will be on (*Gives yesterday's date*)

MAN: That was yesterday.

WALTER: Exactly! Yesterday!

MAN: No Nostradamus, are you?

WALTER: I'll bid you a good night. *Hear ye all, the end is upon us!*

WOMAN: Roger, has he gone?

MAN: Yeah, he's gone. He's really gone!

An eBay Bargain

'Flogging his wheelchair? Must be strapped for cash if he's getting rid of that!'

INTRODUCTION

It's always amazed me to read reports of some of the things people manage to sell on eBay. Still, I suppose we all like a bargain. Just imagine that a paralysed man, who has been in a wheelchair all his life, is suddenly healed and able to walk perfectly well. What would he do with his now surplus-to-requirements wheelchair? Flog it on eBay, of course!

Characters: NORMAN; GEOFF; DAPHNE (doing newspaper crossword).

NORM: I tell you what, Geoff, my Daphne is a genius.

GEOFF: Oh, is she now?

NORM: Yeah, a right little brain-box if ever there was one. Isn't that right, love?

DAPHNE: Yeah, love, whatever you say.

NORM: We were watching that *Countdown* the other day, and she only went and got a four-letter word! Isn't that right, love?

DAPHNE: Yeah.

GEOFF: That was very impressive, Daphne.

NORM: Too right it was! What was the word again, love?

DAPHNE: Nerd.

NORM: Eh?

DAPHNE: Nerd. That was the word.

NORM: Course it was, yeah. Nerd. Good, eh Geoff? (*Spells letters*) N I R D – nerd.

GEOFF: (*Pause*) It's N E R D.

NORM: You what?

GEOFF: Nerd is N E R D, not N I R D.

NORM: Is that right, now?

GEOFF: 'Fraid so.

NORM: Did you hear that, love?

DAPHNE: Yeah.

NORM: I suppose Carol Vorderman's job's safe for a bit, then.

DAPHNE: I suppose so.

NORM: You're pretty impressive with your spellings there, Geoff. Maybe you should go on *Countdown*.

GEOFF: No, I couldn't.

NORM: Course you could.

GEOFF: It's the lights. It's easy in your front room, but a whole different game in a studio with all those lights.

NORM: Oh, come on! A spelling whizz like you – you'd walk away with more than the consolation dictionary and t-shirt.

GEOFF: I don't think so, Norman.

NORM: Imagine the kind of saddo that would wear a t-shirt with *Countdown* on it!

GEOFF: That would be pretty tragic.

NORM: Mind you, could be worth a few bob.

GEOFF: What, a scruffy old t-shirt?

NORM: Collectors' item, that, Geoff. You remember that show *Bullseye*?

GEOFF: The darts one with Jim Bowen?

DAPHNE: Ooh, I loved that show.

NORM: Well, I wasn't asking you. Anyway, do you remember that the consolation prize for the loser was a bendy bully?

GEOFF: Yeah, I remember – load of tripe, wasn't it?

NORM: That's as maybe. Collectors' item now – very rare.

GEOFF: You're joking!

NORM: I kid you not. I saw one on that eBay – you'll never guess how much.

GEOFF: No idea.

NORM: Have a guess.

GEOFF: A tenner.

NORM: Higher.

GEOFF: Twenty.

NORM: No. I'll tell you – seventy-five quid.

GEOFF: Seventy-five quid! Amazing!

NORM: They sell some stuff on that eBay, don't they?

GEOFF: They certainly do.

NORM: There was one chap on there, and you will not believe what he had up for sale.

GEOFF: Go on, then.

NORM: I can hardly bring myself to say it – his family! No word of a lie – 'For sale, my family, sensible offers only.'

GEOFF: You can't credit some people.

NORM: He was from America, though. Ohio, I think.

GEOFF: Well, that explains a lot.

NORM: And his starting price was one American dollar! (*Nods towards Daphne*) I'd want at least fifty quid for her.

DAPHNE: Eh, watch it, you!

NORM: Only kidding, love.

GEOFF: I've got something on eBay at the moment.

NORM: Oh yeah? What are you trying to flog?

GEOFF: Well, it's not for me, actually. I'm doing a favour for old Amos.

NORM: Not flogging his wife, is he?

GEOFF: No, his wheelchair.

NORM: His wheelchair? Must be strapped for cash if he's getting rid of that!

GEOFF: He doesn't need it now.

NORM: How's he going to get about, then – float?

GEOFF: Walk, like the rest of us, I guess.

NORM: Walk? We are talking about paralysed Amos, aren't we?

GEOFF: Yes and no.

NORM: Blimey, you're more cryptic than her.

DAPHNE: Cryptic! Yes! 'Confusing clue, seven letters, beginning and ending with a C.' Thanks. Sorry, carry on.

GEOFF: What I mean is, yes it's that Amos, but no he's not paralysed, not any more.

NORM: Well, how did that come about?

GEOFF: He's been healed. By that speaker bloke.

NORM: What speaker bloke?

GEOFF: You know – the one who did that talk the other week about blessing the meek and the mourners and the hungry.

NORM: Oh, him!

DAPHNE: Jesus.

NORM: No need to swear, love.

DAPHNE: That's his name, dopey!

NORM: Oh, so it is. And he's healed old Amos?

GEOFF: Apparently so.

NORM: Not even a limp?

GEOFF: Nope. Could run a marathon.

NORM: Unbelievable. Life never ceases to amaze me. I'll have to track down this Jesus.

DAPHNE: What, to see if he can heal your piles?

NORM: No. I might see if I can get an autograph. Might be worth a few bob one day on eBay.

GEOFF: You never know.

DAPHNE: You and your eBay!

NORM: Oh, pipe down! What are you up to over there, anyway?

DAPHNE: A crossword.

NORM: Tricky one, is it?

DAPHNE: No, it's just the twenty-minute teabreak one.

NORM: And how long you been at it?

DAPHNE: Four and a half hours.

NORM: Oh, for goodness' sake, give yourself a rest and make a pot of tea. The tongue is literally hanging out of poor Geoff.

DAPHNE: (*Exits*) Yes, master.

NORM: (*Sighs*) I tell you, Geoff, some people don't know they're born!

BIBLE REFERENCE
Matthew 9:1–8

A Far-Fetched Story

'His story begins with some poor chap having seven kinds of wind
kicked out of him by a bunch of robbers'

INTRODUCTION

This monologue is based on the parable of the Good Samaritan. I
read a fascinating book about the parables that took into account
the cultural nuances of the time that are totally alien to us. This
informed my thinking in writing this and should get the audience
asking a few important questions.

Character: MAN.

MAN: Most stories, I find, have a strong and very engaging
opening, but before long it's inevitable they will go
beyond the bounds of all logic and reason. It's as if you're
being lulled into a false sense of security, only to have
your expectations dashed and disappointed minutes later.
And this was very much the case with the event I want to
recall to you now. One of my highly esteemed colleagues,
an expert in matters relating to the law, asked this rather
controversial new teacher by the name of Jesus what the
Scriptures meant by the phrase, 'Love your neighbour.'
Or, to put it another way, who is my neighbour?

     Very cleverly, this Jesus shirked the issue and went into
one of those deep and meaningful stories of his, all about
a lot of stuff and nonsense, in reality meaning very little.

His story begins with some poor chap having seven kinds of wind kicked out of him by a bunch of robbers while travelling between Jerusalem and Jericho. This group of bandits leave him stripped naked and half-beaten to death. Fair start to a story, I suppose – no complaints so far.

Now, first on the scene is a priest who, Jesus said, happened to be going down the same road. Well, there was no 'happened' about it, I can tell you! That road is seventeen miles of arduous desert, so there was obviously a point to his journey, and the point probably was that he was on his way home from work. He had more than likely completed his two-week shift at the temple in Jerusalem and was now travelling back home to Jericho for a well-earned rest. Well, what do you expect him to do when faced with an apparently dead body? If he touches a body that turns out to be deceased, he'll be defiled. He'll have to traipse all the way back up to Jerusalem and go through some long-winded purification ritual. And by the time he's done that, it'll be pointless going back home at all, 'cos he'll be back on shift again! 'And anyway,' the priest would have thought, 'this man may have been a sinner, so why should I help? There he is, totally naked, no clothes to identify his ethnic race or belief system. Surely our law urges us not to help sinners!' So it's understandable that he passed by on the other side. Cast the poor priest as a villain if you will, but I see him as a victim of his own cherished rule-book, trapped, if you like, by an unwavering belief in his ethical and theological system. With me so far?

Anyway, next on the scene is a Levite – one who, as a teacher of the law, would doubtless look up to the priest. Now, that desert road, the one between Jerusalem and Jericho, is not only very long but also very flat. So it's highly likely that this Levite had clocked the priest travelling ahead of him. So when he comes across this poor chap all beaten and bruised, what's he gonna think? Surely, if the high and mighty priest has ignored this bloke and passed by, why shouldn't he do the same? It's not that he doesn't care, he just doesn't see it as his problem.

So at this stage, the story, as far as we were concerned, seemed okey-dokey. We're just waiting now for the inevitable third traveller, the one who offers help, the one who was obviously going to be of the Jewish persuasion! Or so we thought. In fact, this is the part of the story where, from my point of view, things get a bit silly. For who is it that emerges through the desert's shimmering light to tend to the victim and pour oil on his wounds but a Samaritan! A hated and hateful Samaritan. I mean, as if! If a Samaritan had come along, he would have probably put the boot in a bit more, even while the bloke was lying down. A Samaritan! Of all the images Jesus could have used to portray compassion and a gut-level reaction to others' suffering, he chooses a Samaritan!

I'll give this Jesus credit for bravery – making our sworn enemy the hero of his story was never likely to win him a horde of admirers.

When Jesus asked my colleague who he thought the neighbour was, he just replied, 'The one who had mercy.' He couldn't bear to say the 's' word. I guess Jesus wasn't so much asking 'Who was the neighbour?' as 'Who must you be a neighbour to?'

Funny, really. Still, it was only a story, I suppose. And a far-fetched one at that. Ludicrously far-fetched.

BIBLE REFERENCE
Luke 10:25–37

The Professional Mourner

'Thank you, darling. I've been perfecting that particular whimper for over a decade'

INTRODUCTION

Here's one of my favourite sketches – not sure why, but I think it's a combination of general silliness and a glorious opportunity to do some extremely hammy acting! I read something about people in ancient times being employed as mourners and thought that it might be a perfect job for a failed or has-been actor. What if the mourner was employed at a funeral when, all of a sudden, the deceased was no longer deceased? Enter Lazarus. . .

Characters: REGINALD; TOM.

REG: (*Various groans and wails*)

TOM: (*Quietly*) Hello there.

REG: Ah, hello, young man!

TOM: Sorry to interrupt you in full flow.

REG: No problem at all – just fine-tuning the instrument. No such thing as too much practice in my line.

TOM: No, I'm sure not.

REG: Haven't seen you around before. New, are you?

TOM: Yes, first day – just trying to learn the ropes.

REG: Ah well, feel free to observe, dear boy – been in the game nearly thirty years now. I'm sure I could teach you a trick or two.

TOM: Well, that's very kind, if you're sure you don't mind.

REG: Not at all, 'tis my pleasure. We professional mourners need to stick together. We're rather a dying breed – if you catch my drift!

TOM: (*Misses joke*) I beg your pardon?

REG: Dying breed. My little joke – do you get it?

TOM: Oh yes, I see. Very amusing – do forgive me.

REG: Think nothing of it – just a little jest to help the day go by. So what got you into the mourning game, then?

TOM: Oh, I failed my GCSEs, so they put me on one of these youth enterprise schemes to help me learn a trade.

REG: Well, you couldn't have chosen a better vocation, my dear boy. Mourning has brought me years of joy. I know that sounds rather paradoxical, but there you are.

TOM: And quite easy, they tell me.

REG: *Easy?* Never! Not if you want to be well respected and at the top of your trade. Your whole career will be a learning curve. I still consider myself an apprentice to the art.

TOM: Oh dear – they told me all I had to do was moan and groan a bit.

REG: Moan and groan a bit? Typical! Well, I suppose if you want to do a shoddy job you can get away with it. Take Barry Simpson – been in the trade the best part of twenty years and his mourning still sounds like a very slight tummy-ache.

TOM: That sounds very unprofessional.

REG: Precisely, young man. It's cowboys like him who give our trade a bad name.

TOM: So what kind of service do you provide?

REG: Well, that depends on the budget of the client, my dear boy. For a basic pauper's funeral I avail myself to the clients just for the funeral procession and burial. My role is simply to whimper and groan in a surreptitious manner. Let me demonstrate. (*REG whimpers and groans fairly quietly in a theatrical manner*)

TOM: Wow! That was fantastic!

REG: Thank you, darling. I've been perfecting that particular whimper for over a decade.

TOM: And what about the next level up?

REG: With the medium package I stay for the whole day, and my whimpers and groans are upgraded to a more cacophonous wail with the addition of real tears.

TOM: Real tears?

REG: Yes, I know – impressive, isn't it? I will demonstrate as best as I can, though real tears can only be summoned on the day of performance, so to speak. (*REG theatrically wails and sobs*)

TOM: You're amazing! I'll never be able to do that.

REG: Fear not, my dear boy, with my training you will be amazed at what you can achieve.

TOM: Well, maybe. Did you say that was only medium?

REG: Oh yes. My luxury service can often last a week, as I attend all the proceedings, including the wake. I also increase the level of wails to a riotous level, accompanied by occasional rolling around on the ground – though I've had to limit that recently, as I've been struck with lumbago.

TOM: Can I get a preview?

REG: I'll do my best, though for this level, preparation is paramount. (*REG wails and sobs, rolling on floor*)

TOM: Sir, I'm dumbstruck. You really are awe-inspiring.

REG: Most kind of you to say so.

TOM: I'm sure all your clients are delighted with your services.

REG: Indeed they are. Thirty years and never a bad review.

TOM: That's quite a testimony – no dissatisfied customers in all that time.

REG: None! Actually, I tell a lie. About a year ago I did have a setback to my good professional name.

TOM: What happened?

REG: Well, I'd been employed by two lovely local sisters to mourn for their recently departed brother. Mary and Martha were their names, I believe.

TOM: And what happened?

REG: Everything had gone swimmingly well. I'd wailed during the procession and sobbed at the burial, conducting the whole funeral party into a mourning frenzy.

TOM: Sounds like a good day at the office.

REG: Yes, but after four days' mourning outside the tomb, one of the friends of the deceased turned up. Can't have been that close, I thought, not turning up for the funeral. Anyway – would you believe this? – he called out for the stone of the tomb to be rolled back!

TOM: After four days?

REG: Precisely! Well, the sisters warned him what the smell would be from a rotting corpse, but he insisted. So the stone was rolled back and he summoned the poor man – Lazarus was his name, if memory serves – to 'come out!'

TOM: And what happened then?

REG: He came out. Strips of linen hanging off his hands and feet, a mouldy old cloth around his face.

TOM: So he was alive?

REG: Apparently so. I wasn't really watching. I'm a professional, so I was scrabbling around in the gravel, wailing to the heavens.

TOM: Sounds like a bit of a miracle. Who was this friend?

REG: I've no idea who he was, and it was most certainly not a miracle. The sisters, delighted with their newly breathing brother, rushed over to me and told me to stop mourning! Me, a professional mourner! They asked if I could change tack and start laughing and cheering instead.

TOM: And did you?

REG: I most certainly did not! Laughing and cheering are not part of my repertoire, which I politely explained to them.

They then forthwith dispensed with my services. My good name besmirched forever!

TOM: And what happened to Lazarus and this mystery friend?

REG: I've no idea, I'm afraid, or any interest. People coming back from the dead is very bad for our business, very bad indeed.

TOM: Doesn't happen much, though, I suppose.

REG: Very seldom, I'm sure, very seldom indeed.

BIBLE REFERENCE
John chapter 11

The Lost Sheep

'Typical! She's probably wandered off to find herself a handsome ram. She really is old mutton dressed as lamb!'

INTRODUCTION

We hear a lot about the lost sheep that the shepherd dutifully goes off to find. But what about the other ninety-nine? What did they get up to while the shepherd went on his search? And what did they think of the lost sheep?

Characters: MATILDA; JOYCE.

Sound effects of sheep baa-ing.

MATILDA: Hello, Joyce, how are you?

JOYCE: Oh, fine thanks, Matilda. Haven't seen you for a while.

MATILDA: No, I've been tootling along at the back, but now we've stopped I thought I'd mingle a bit.

JOYCE: Well, it's lovely to see you. How's Arthur?

MATILDA: Oh, not too good at the mo. He's managed to contract hoof rot. Hobbling about like an old age pensioner, he is. That's why I'm stuck at the back.

JOYCE: Oh dear! Do send him my regards, won't you?

MATILDA: Will do. And how about your Wilfred?

JOYCE: Very well, thank you. Just having a snooze at the moment. Ooh, except that he's suddenly gone as bald as a coot.

MATILDA:	No!
JOYCE:	Yes, no word of a lie.
MATILDA:	Oh, what a shame, Joycie. I mean, going bald, it's such a social embarrassment, isn't it?
JOYCE:	Don't I know it!
MATILDA:	How did it happen?
JOYCE:	The shepherd boy takes him off the other day. Next thing I know, Wilfred's gone bald and the shepherd's wearing this lovely woolly jersey.
MATILDA:	Really? Sounds like there should be an obvious connection there. Shame we sheep are too thick to work out things like that.
JOYCE:	Yes, one of the many perils of our species, I'm afraid.
MATILDA:	The sun's baking hot today, isn't it?
JOYCE:	It is – gives me the most terrible migraines.
MATILDA:	Oh, poor ewe. Oh, do you get it? Poor ewe! Oh, forget it.
JOYCE:	It's no joke. I couldn't sleep last night. Tossing and turning all over the place, I was. Wilfred got the right old hump.
MATILDA:	You must be shattered, love.
JOYCE:	I tried to drop off by closing my eyes and counting humans.
MATILDA:	That's a novel idea. Did you get very far?
JOYCE:	No, I can't count.
MATILDA:	Shame. Anyway, have you got any idea what the hold-up is? We don't usually get a mid-afternoon break.
JOYCE:	Haven't you heard?
MATILDA:	Heard what?
JOYCE:	About Judith.
MATILDA:	Oh, Judith. What about her?
JOYCE:	She's wandered off, hasn't she? The old shepherd boy was doing his count-up, realises he's only got

ninety-nine. One's done a runner. And guess who it is – Judith!

MATILDA: Well, that's typical, isn't it? Probably wandered off trying to find herself a handsome ram. Ooh, she really is mutton dressed up as lamb.

JOYCE: The shepherd boy must rate her, mustn't he? He's gone rushing off to find her and left us ninety-nine hanging around here like a bunch of lemons.

MATILDA: I call that favouritism. Imagine if it had been your Wilfred who'd wandered off – do you think he would have gone rushing after him?

JOYCE: Not now he's a right old baldy-head. He'd probably be happy to get shot of him.

MATILDA: Poor thing. It's wicked to mock the afflicted.

JOYCE: But if a sheep wanders off, it's their look-out. Let them go and be done with them.

MATILDA: I agree. It's a lot of fuss for one sheep, especially Judith.

JOYCE: Hello – talk of the devil! Here she is – the shepherd boy's got her slung over his shoulders.

MATILDA: Blimey, take a look at her – atomic mutton! She really is an embarrassment to our species.

JOYCE: And look at the smile on his face now he's found her! Easily pleased, isn't he? I mean, how can you get so euphoric over one lost sheep?

MATILDA: Well, it's obvious isn't it? He's simple. Not a brain between his ears for individual rational thought.

JOYCE: Exactly. Ooh look, we're on the move, Matilda.

MATILDA: Oh, so we are. I'd better find Arthur. Follow on quickly, Joyce, follow on. . .

BIBLE REFERENCE
Matthew chapter 18

The Dumb Question

'Isn't that the dumbest thing you've ever heard?'

Characters: ONE; TWO; THREE.

THREE is reading a newspaper as ONE and TWO enter, arguing.

ONE: I don't believe it. I still just do not believe it!

TWO: Will you stop going on about it?

ONE: Come on, you must admit it's about the dumbest thing ever.

TWO: It wasn't dumb. It was the best I could do at short notice.

ONE: Best he could do!

TWO: Anyway, you're not exactly the sharpest tool in the box, are you?

ONE: And what's that supposed to mean?

TWO: Come on, what about the time Mr Fergus, our old maths teacher, asked you the answer to 3a minus 2b?

ONE: Here we go again.

TWO: And you said, 'I don't do letters sir, only numbers.'

ONE: That was years ago.

TWO: I know. Still, pretty dumb, though, wasn't it?

ONE: Whatever.

THREE: You two finished arguing yet?

ONE: We're not arguing, we're discussing. In fact you can resolve the debate for us.

THREE: Oh, don't drag me into this.

ONE: Come on, no wimping out. You will not believe what this muppet has just done.

THREE: Should I listen to this?

TWO: You know what he's like. Once he's got a bee in his bonnet there's no stopping him.

THREE: Okay then, shoot.

ONE: Good. Well, we were hanging out with John as usual, trying to fathom what he was going on about, when all of a sudden who should walk by?

THREE: No idea.

ONE: Have a guess.

THREE: Oh, I don't know, Emperor Caesar.

ONE: No, don't be so daft. What would he be doing down here?

TWO: Just get on with it, will you?

ONE: Shut up! Oh, I've lost my place now.

THREE: You're chatting with John and some mysterious person appears.

ONE: Oh yeah. So all of a sudden John declares, 'Look, the lamb of God!'

THREE: You're kidding.

ONE: No, honestly – it's Jesus, the one he's been going on about taking away the sins of the world.

THREE: Did you speak to him?

ONE: Aha, that's where it gets interesting. Dopey over here suggests we go over and try to talk to him.

THREE: Sounds like a good idea.

ONE: Yeah, agreed so far. Slight problem, though – dopey hasn't thought through exactly what to say.

TWO: I told you, it was short notice.

THREE: So what happened?

ONE: Well, we rush over to catch him up, a bit nervous, like, and he must have this extra sense, 'cos he knew we were there. So he turns around and says it.

THREE: Says what?

ONE: 'What do you want?' Just imagine the Chosen One asking what we want! We could ask him anything – all those questions we've discussed on rainy nights, like why all the suffering?

THREE: What about other races?

ONE: Doesn't science disprove God?

THREE: Why is the England football team so pants?

ONE: Exactly – and what does Professor Einstein here come up with?

THREE: Come on then.

ONE: 'Where are you staying?'

THREE: You're kidding.

TWO: I told you, it was short notice.

ONE: Isn't that the dumbest thing you've ever heard?

TWO: I didn't notice you chip in with a deep and probing question.

ONE: I didn't get a chance, thanks to your nincompoopery!

TWO: Come on – you were star-struck and didn't know what to say.

ONE: Which is infinitely preferable to asking, 'Where are you staying?'

THREE: Hang on a sec – maybe it's not such a bad question.

ONE: Oh, not you as well!

THREE: Well, suppose there's a bit more to this than just some pat answers to common questions?

ONE: What are you dribbling on about?

THREE: Perhaps this step of faith isn't just in the mind but in an act of will – a journey, if you like.

ONE: Blimey, have you been eating cous-cous?

TWO: Oh, shut up and listen!

THREE: And if it's a journey, we need to find out a lot more from this guy, don't you think?

TWO: A Solomon in our midst, a wise Solomon!

THREE: So, perhaps finding out where he's staying is not such a dumb question after all.

TWO: My thinking exactly.

ONE: Yeah, amazing what you can come up with at short notice.

BIBLE REFERENCE

John 1:35–38

The Unruly Tenants

'Off you go, spam 'ead, and tell your master, his grapes are our grapes!'

INTRODUCTION

This piece I've used as a two-part sketch, and part two can be revisited at a later stage in the service. It is a stylised look at the parable of the tenants that attempts to raise a few laughs as well as pack a powerful punch.

Characters: ONE; TWO; NARRATOR; SERVANT; MASTER.

PART ONE

NARR: There once was a man – a good, trusting and rich man – who decided to go on holiday, but he had a vineyard and needed some people to look after it while he was away. He made clear to his tenants they would be well paid and treated more than fairly. He trusted that they would look after his business, so off he went.

(*ONE and TWO enter, drunk and singing loudly*)

ONE/TWO: 'Best job in the world, best job in the world, we have got the, we have got the best job in the world!'

ONE: There we were, sitting in The Five Loaves –

TWO: – our local pub –

ONE: – enjoying a pint of Caesar's Black Label –

TWO: – watching the footie –

ONE: – when this geezer comes in.

TWO: 'E says, 'You boys wanna job?'

ONE: 'What do we want one of them for?' I says.

TWO: One word, 'e says – *vino*.

ONE: (*Singing to the theme of 'Food, Glorious Food'*) 'Wine, luvverly wine, la, la la la, la la!'

TWO: 'Here's the deal,' 'e says. 'Work on my vineyard while I'm away and you'll be suitably reimbursed.'

ONE: But he never came back, did he?

TWO: And now it's harvest time, and no sign of our man – probably eaten by a mountain lion or something.

ONE: So we have all the wine we could ever wish for!

TWO: Enough Merlot to keep us mullered until May Day.

ONE: Enough Chardonnay to keep us chucking up till Christmas.

TWO: Enough Pinot Noir to keep us –

ONE: (*Interrupts*) Careful!

ONE/TWO: (*Both laugh and start singing again*)

NARR: The master of the vineyard, however, was not lunch for lions, but fine and well-tanned after a lovely trip to the Canaries. He timed his return to perfection – harvest at his vineyard. So he sent his willing and dutiful servant to collect what was rightfully his.

(*SERVANT enters*)

ONE: 'Ello! What do we have here, then?

TWO: A stranger in The Five Loaves.

ONE: What football team do you support?

SERV: Er, you could say I follow the Jerusalem Artichokes.

ONE: The Jeru– (*Laughs*)

TWO: (*Sings, like a football chant*) 'What a load of rubbish!'

ONE: So what do you want, anyway?

SERV: Well, it's a pleasure to meet my master's willing workers. I am here on behalf of your employer, the owner of the vineyard, which you seem to be, er, enjoying. But it's time to collect the harvest.

ONE: Oh really? So he comes swanning back from his trendy gap year, and expects us to give up the fruits of our hard labour, just like that.

SERV: Well, they are his grapes, and I'm sure you'll be given generous remuneration.

TWO: Renumer-nothin', matey! We're very happy here, and we have no intention of parting with our hard-earned grapes, not a single one. Now get out of here!

SERV: I'm afraid I really must insist.

ONE: Insist? You and whose army? Ahab's?

TWO: Gideon's?

ONE: Hezekiah's?

SERV: Look, I don't want any trouble – just give him what is rightfully his.

ONE: (*Menacingly*) Listen, mate, that's a lovely nose you've got there. Almost Roman, you could say. Now if you want to keep it that way I suggest you leave.

TWO: Off you go, spam 'ead, and tell your master, his grapes are our grapes.

SERV: But –

ONE: Leave!

(*SERVANT exits*)

ONE/TWO: (*Laugh and sing*) 'We are the champions!'

NARR: And so the servant returned to his master, grapeless, and the locals at The Five Loaves celebrated a great victory with a few glasses of – yes, you've guessed, wine. But they had not seen the end of the master yet. What would he try next? Would The Five Loaves thugs be victorious? Find out in part two. . .

PART TWO

NARR: Back to the story. The master was not best pleased with the locals at The Five Loaves who had decided to relieve him of the fruit from his vineyards. Neither was he content with his servant's ineffectual harvest-collecting. So he sent him back a second time, and a third time. . .

(*SERVANT enters, battered and bruised*)

MASTER: Ah, there you are, Weatherspoon! I'm sure you have some lovely grapes for me this time. (*Notices injuries*) What have they done to you, you poor man?

SERV: No real problem, sir. This time after the statutory stoning with mouldy, maggot-infested grapes, they decided to juice me, sir.

MASTER: Juice you? Whatever does that mean?

SERV: Well, I was thrown in the wine press and battered senseless by twelve drunken louts.

MASTER: Oh, that is beyond the pale! Have they no respect?

SERV: Er, apparently not! To tell you the truth, they're getting worse. If I go back again they say they'll kill me.

MASTER: Kill you?

SERV: Yes. And I believe them, sir.

MASTER: Well, thank you, Weatherspoon. I'm sorry for your trials. I think you had best go and rest up.

SERV: Thank you, sir. (*Exits*)

NARR: So the master thought about who he could send that would deliver the message with his own authority. Someone they would respect. There was only one choice – his son, his own flesh and blood. The exact representation of the father. Surely they would treat him well. . .

(*During this speech the MASTER takes off his cloak and becomes the SON. ONE and TWO enter*)

ONE: Ah, look who it is! It's his son. That stupid, trusting fool of a master.

TWO: As if it's going to make any difference to us who he sends.

ONE: Now we have him. Do away with the son and the inheritance is ours!

TWO: Set up for life.

ONE: Just by killing him.

TWO: (*Sarcastically to the son*) Son of the master, think you're something special, do you?

ONE: You don't need to say a word, we know the story.

TWO: Your beloved father sends you down here to deal with us.

ONE: Surely we will obey his son!

TWO: His own flesh and blood. What with him being so generous and all.

ONE: Well, he was wrong.

TWO: Very, very wrong.

ONE: And you won't be seeing him to tell him his mistake.

TWO: You see, we know the end of this little story.

NARR: And the men took the innocent son and killed him. (*ONE and TWO beat up the SON, kneeing him in the stomach and then pulling him up to form the shape of the cross*) The father had placed his trust in these men, and they had betrayed him in the worst possible way.

(*Optional end is for the NARRATOR to read Isaiah 53:7*)

BIBLE REFERENCE
Mark 12: 1–9

Pigs in Love

'Stone the living crows, it's a bloomin' stampede! Now they're all going in for a dip!'

INTRODUCTION

I'm not particularly an animal lover, but the story in Luke chapter 8, where the demons are sent into a herd of pigs, has always struck me as a bit unfair! Here we get the story from the perspective of a couple of young pigs having an illicit affair and witnessing the mass surge into the river of all their relatives.

Characters: HENRY; CLARISSA.

(*HENRY is onstage, snorting and restless; CLARISSA joins him*)

CLARISSA: Psst! Psst!

HENRY: Oh, there you are, darling!

CLARISSA: You managed to sneak off, then?

HENRY: Yeah – did anyone spot you coming up?

CLARISSA: I don't think so – they were all too busy with their snouts stuck in that trough of slops.

HENRY: Oh, they really are a bunch of pigs, aren't they?

CLARISSA: Well, you can take the pig out of the farmyard, but you can't take the farmyard out of the pig.

HENRY: Well, it suits us, darling. As ever, you look utterly ravishing.

CLARISSA: Thank you, Henry darling, and you smell absolutely divine. What is it?

HENRY: Horse excrement, I think. Lovely, isn't it?

CLARISSA: Mmm, makes my trotters go all tingly.

HENRY: Oh, Clarissa, being with you makes me complete. It makes me so happy I could 'sing to the world'!

CLARISSA: Henry, calm down, for goodness' sake – they'll spot us, you great lump of gammon!

HENRY: I'm sorry but I can't help myself. When are we going to come clean and declare our love to the world?

CLARISSA: Darling, you know we can't – not now, at least. We're doomed, star-crossed lovers.

HENRY: It's so dashed unfair.

CLARISSA: Yes, I know, but you were born from a rather unimpressive lower-caste litter. It's a case of economics.

HENRY: Yes, I know – don't rub it in. But in these enlightened times surely we can rise above all that class nonsense?

CLARISSA: Maybe at some stage we can, but at the moment you know how daddy is.

HENRY: Oh, don't talk to me about the general!

CLARISSA: Well, you need to watch out for him. He told me that if he catches me with any pig outside our caste, he'll arrange for us both to be turned into pork scratchings.

HENRY: Pork scratchings? What are they?

CLARISSA: I don't know, but they sound painful.

HENRY: So we just have to make do with our private little rendezvous?

CLARISSA: For now, I'm afraid so.

HENRY: Well, it could be worse, I suppose. And true love always finds a way!

CLARISSA: That's the spirit, darling.

HENRY: So how are things on your side of the hill at the moment?

CLARISSA: Much the same, you know. We've still got that crazy human scaring the living daylights out of us.

HENRY: Oh yes, how so?

CLARISSA: Well, I think he's lost his marbles. He's taken to liv-
            ing in the tombs just by our sty, and runs about all
            day completely (*Mimes being naked*).

HENRY: I beg your pardon?

CLARISSA: (*Embarrassed*) You know – naked!

HENRY: Naked? Well, I don't see the problem with that. I mean,
            we're always naked, aren't we? It's only natural.

CLARISSA: Yes, Henry, but we're pigs! It's different for him –
            he's human. It's just not – pleasant.

HENRY: Fair point, I suppose.

CLARISSA: Humans just don't know how to control themselves.
            And they have the cheek to call *us* pigs!

HENRY: (*Pause. HENRY looks, confused, into the distance*) I didn't
            know your daddy was a swimmer.

CLARISSA: Daddy, a swimmer? What are you talking about – he
            hates the water.

HENRY: Well, he's just gone for a dip, I'm telling you. Looks
            like a few others are following him, too.

CLARISSA: Where?

HENRY: By the water, of course, dopey! Down there!

CLARISSA: Oh, I can't see all the way down there, not without
            my glasses. Are you sure it's daddy?

HENRY: Stone the living crows, it's a blooming stampede!
            Now they're all going for a dip.

CLARISSA: Oh, stop exaggerating, Henry!

HENRY: I'm not! They are literally all going into the sea –
            even my old granny!

CLARISSA: Your granny! Oh, this is daft – the whole piggy pop-
            ulation of the Gerasenes gone swimming! If they're
            not careful they'll all drown themselves.

HENRY: Don't say that, Clarissa! Don't even think it.

CLARISSA: Well, just imagine it. The whole pig population
            totally wiped out in one afternoon – except for us.

HENRY: Scary thought.

CLARISSA: It would be down to us and us alone to subdue the
            earth and revive the pig population. The survival of
            the species would depend on us.

HENRY: (*Pause*) Tiring thought. Very tiring.

CLARISSA: Any of them out of the water yet?

HENRY: No, doesn't look like it. All still in there. . .

BIBLE REFERENCE

Luke 8: 26–39

A New High Priest

'We're no longer needed. Surplus to requirements – defunct!'

INTRODUCTION

So, with the arrival of a new High Priest, what happens to all the old ones? All of a sudden they find themselves surplus to requirements. Must have been quite some queue at the jobcentre!

Characters: STACY; EZRA.

STACY is sitting at her desk, talking on the phone.

STACY: No, tell him he needs to fill in a DS 142. . . I don't care if he is a high-flier, Marge, he's still got to fill it in. . . No, it isn't pink, it's green! You've got a DF 142 there, you daft moose. The DF 142 is pink, the DS 142 is green. Got it?. . . Okay, see you later, love. (*Puts phone down. To herself*) What would they do without me?
Next client, please!

EZRA: That's me, I think, miss.

STACY: Good afternoon, sir, and welcome to the Samarian branch of your friendly DSS. My name is Stacy. How may I facilitate you today?

EZRA: Well, I need to know how to go about finding new employment.

STACY: Oh dear, lost your job recently, have you?

EZRA: Yes, very recently.

STACY: What, push you out 'cos you're a bit long in the tooth, did they?

EZRA: No, nothing like that. I was made redundant – lots of us
        were.

STACY: More cutbacks, I suppose? Sign of the times, I'm afraid.

EZRA: Sort of. Well, actually it was – it was – Jesus Christ.

STACY: There's no need to swear, sir! I'm a government official –
        I've had to deal with your sort before.

EZRA: No, you misunderstand. Jesus Christ is the reason I've
        been made redundant.

STACY: Oh, I see. What was your job, then?

EZRA: I was a High Priest.

STACY: He after that job, then, is he?

EZRA: Apparently so – he's the new Great High Priest. We're no
        longer needed. Surplus to requirements – defunct!

STACY: Oh, come on, now, don't be so hard on yourself. I'm sure
        you have lots of abilities. We can soon sort you out with
        another suitable career.

EZRA: What do you suggest, then?

STACY: Let's see. For starters, what kind of skills have you
        learned in your previous employment?

EZRA: I'm very good at making offerings.

STACY: Offerings?

EZRA: Yes, you know, burnt offerings, grain offerings, fellow-
        ship offerings, sin offerings, guilt offerings –

STACY: That sounds interesting.

EZRA: Yes, very popular. I did a particularly good line in guilt
        offerings – everyone likes a good dose of guilt.

STACY: That's all very well, but I'm not sure that all those offer-
        ings are a directly transferable skills base.

EZRA: Meaning?

STACY: Well, meaning that when it comes to getting another job
        I don't think those skills are going to do you much good.

EZRA: (*Annoyed*) But I've perfected them over many years! It's
        not just anybody that can do this kind of work, you
        know.

STACY: Okay, okay, simmer down! I'm only trying to help.

EZRA: I'm sorry. I know you are. It's just been a tough time.

STACY: Look, why don't you tell me what these offerings specifically entail?

EZRA: Well, a variety of tasks – sacrifices, for instance.

STACY: Sacrifices? I don't like the sound of that.

EZRA: Oh, it's very routine. For one sacrifice we slaughter an animal at the entrance of the tent, sprinkle some blood about, take the fat that covers the inner parts and both kidneys with fat near the loins, remove the kidneys and burn them.

STACY: All right, all right, I've just had my lunch!

EZRA: Oh, sorry.

STACY: Well, there's not much call for those, er, services nowadays. I can't think what we can possibly. . . (*Moment of inspiration*) Wait a moment! Have you considered butchery?

EZRA: Butchery?

STACY: A very solid job, that. People will always want meat.

EZRA: I don't want to be awkward, but I don't agree with eating certain animals – my religion, you understand.

STACY: Oh, I see. How about a kosher butcher?

EZRA: It's just not me. I was a man of some standing, you see.

STACY: Oh, now you're just being fussy. You do realise that if you refuse any reasonable job we can withhold all benefits?

EZRA: I don't wish to be unreasonable. It's just that the priesthood is all I've ever done.

STACY: Are you sure you can't stick with it? Maybe this Jesus will need some helpers – he can't do it all himself, can he?

EZRA: That may be true.

STACY: That's the spirit! I mean, what can he offer that you can't?

EZRA: (*Pause, thoughtfully*) He's gone through the clouds of heaven. He is able to sympathise with our every weakness. He has been tempted in every way possible yet remained sinless. In him alone we can approach the throne of grace with confidence, utter confidence.

STACY: Sounds impressive.

EZRA: Oh, he is. He is.

STACY: Yes. . . I think I'd better get you a form to fill in. You'll be needing form DS 142 – it's the green one.

BIBLE REFERENCE
Hebrews 4:14

Bring and Buy

'I've picked up a Robert Ludlum book for my Charlie – he does love a good thriller'

Characters: JOAN; MABEL; LINDA; SANDRA.

JOAN is onstage rooting through her handbag. LINDA is behind her stall to one side of the stage. MABEL enters and goes to JOAN.

MABEL: Ooh, hello, Joany love.

JOAN: Oh, there you are, Mabel. I was wondering where you'd got to.

MABEL: Sorry, dear, I got held up at the tombola – bit of a queue.

JOAN: Had a bit of a gamble, did you?

MABEL: I know, a little devil, aren't I? Not very Christian, is it, gambling at a church do, but it's all for a good cause.

JOAN: Well, that makes it worthwhile, doesn't it?

MABEL: Yes, exactly.

JOAN: What is the good cause it's all in aid of?

MABEL: Eh? Oh, I don't know, truth be told. Think it's something to do with foreign people.

JOAN: Oh lovely – that's very worthwhile, then, isn't it?

MABEL: Well, I'm the first person to put my hand in my pocket for a good cause, Joany.

JOAN: So did you win anything in the tombola?

MABEL: Sort of. Do you know the cheeky wotsits were charging twenty pence a ticket? Twenty pence!

JOAN: That's not bad if you get a winner.

MABEL: That was the problem – I spent £1.60 to get a winner.

You had to get a ticket ending in a zero or five. Well, I had ones and fours and sixes galore, but it took eight goes to get a five.

JOAN: And what did you win?

MABEL: A tube of talcum powder. I wish I hadn't bothered. Could have bought it for forty pence at Superdrug.

JOAN: Ah, it's all for a good cause, though.

MABEL: I suppose so. What about you – got any bargains?

JOAN: I picked up a Robert Ludlum book for my Charlie – he does love a good thriller.

MABEL: How much did that set you back?

JOAN: Ten pence.

MABEL: Paperback or hardback?

JOAN: Paperback – the hardbacks were thirty pence.

MABEL: Thirty pence? Criminal, isn't it? I'm ready for a cup of tea, Joany. They're probably charging the earth for one of them, too.

JOAN: It's twenty-five pence, including a biscuit.

MABEL: Well, let's get a shift on – hopefully all the jammy dodgers haven't gone!

JOAN: Good thinking!

LINDA: (*Calls from her stall*) Mabel, Joan, yoo-hoo!

MABEL: Oh, lumme, it's Linda Maguire. I was trying to avoid her. She's got a right pile of old tat on her stall.

LINDA: Are you going to come and look at my wares, ladies?

JOAN: Yes, just coming, Linda! Come on, Mabel, it won't harm.

MABEL: Oh, love a duck. (*They walk over*) Ooh, Linda, you've got some lovely things on your stall this year, dear.

LINDA: Well, I try my best. There's always a little prize for who raises most money.

JOAN: You've got a good chance this year, Linda.

LINDA: Thank you, Joan, that's very kind.

MABEL: What's this, Linda love, is it just a bag?

LINDA: No dear, it's a toiletry bag.

MABEL: Oh yes? What's in it, then?

LINDA: Just a few hand lotions, bath gels, that sort of thing.

MABEL: What scent is it?

LINDA: Lilac.

MABEL: Oh, that's no good then – lilac sets off my Arthur's allergies.

LINDA: Oh dear.

MABEL: Yes, I bought a lilac air freshener once – you know, those ones you plug in – and he came up in a huge rash. Repellent, it was.

LINDA: Nasty.

MABEL: What are these?

LINDA: They're little candle-holders.

MABEL: Ooh, natty – but what's all that splodge down the side?

LINDA: My granddaughter decorated them.

MABEL: Oh, beg pardon. What's it supposed to be?

LINDA: They're flowers.

MABEL: Flowers? How old is she?

LINDA: Nearly seven.

MABEL: Well, she's got time to learn, then.

JOAN: Are those mince pies, Linda?

LINDA: Yes, home-made ones. You get a tray of four for seventy-five pence.

JOAN: Go on, then – I'll take a tray.

LINDA: There we are! Thank you, ladies.

MABEL: Bye-bye, Linda. (*They walk away*) Seventy-five pence for four mince pies!

JOAN: That's not too bad, Mabel.

MABEL: Highway robbery! And they're manky home-made ones, not even Mr Kipling's – I ask you!

(*SANDRA enters and starts talking to LINDA*)

JOAN: Well, it's all for a good cause. Look, old Sandra Watkins seems in a bit of a flap.

MABEL: So she does. Looks like she's having one of her hot flushes.

LINDA: *(To SANDRA) She has not!*

JOAN: Ooh, someone's not happy.

MABEL: No. . . Everything okay there, Linda love?

LINDA: Not really, no.

MABEL: Whatever's up, dear?

LINDA: You tell them, Sandra. I can't bear to.

SANDRA: Well, no guesses who was first in today as soon as the fete opened – Mary.

MABEL: Ooh, what a surprise! Snapping up all the bargains, was she?

SANDRA: Just one item, actually. Someone had donated a bottle of this posh new fragrance by Jennifer Lopez – very nice. And not just a little bottle –industrial size, worth a fortune.

MABEL: I hope you charged sensible money for it.

LINDA: It wasn't cheap, especially on her income.

SANDRA: Anyway, I've just heard she's used the whole lot in one go.

MABEL: What? I know she cakes it on but that's ridiculous!

SANDRA: That's the thing – it wasn't on herself. It was this new preacher, teacher fellow going around – what's his name?

LINDA: Jesus.

SANDRA: That's the one. Well, she goes to see him, smashes the bottle and pours the whole lot over his feet!

JOAN: On his feet?

MABEL: I don't suppose he was overly chuffed about having a load of women's perfume chucked over his feet!

SANDRA: He didn't mind at all. In fact he was very moved.

MABEL: There's no accounting for taste, is there?

SANDRA: You're right there, Mabel.

LINDA: You sure you don't want to take this last tray of mince pies off my hands, Mabel?

MABEL: No, we're all right, love. We're just going to grab a tea and jammy dodger, actually.

LINDA: Oh, all the jammy dodgers have gone, love. Only malted milk left now, I'm afraid.

MABEL: Oh, that just about takes the biscuit.

JOAN: Very good Mabel – just about takes the biscuit!

MABEL: Eh? Oh yeah, very funny. Come on. . .

BIBLE REFERENCE
Luke 7:36–50

My Father's House

'My Joe's a carpenter by trade, but we've had a wobbly bookshelf in the lounge for I don't know how long!'

INTRODUCTION

I wrote this sketch at Madrid airport waiting for a return flight to Gatwick. For some reason I was thinking of the story of Mary and Joseph losing Jesus and him turning up in his Father's house. Here's a twist on that story, brought up to date and situated in a bustling airport.

Characters: MARY; JOE.

MARY: Honestly, it's absolutely disgusting!

JOE: Yeah, well, don't keep going on about it.

MARY: Why shouldn't I? It's just plain wrong.

JOE: Yes, we've established that. Now let's move on, shall we?

MARY: £2.19 for a cup of coffee. Unbelievable, isn't it – £2.19!

JOE: Here she goes again.

MARY: Well, are you surprised? It's criminal. And I bet the poor coffee grower only gets a couple of pence.

JOE: Less than that, I should think.

MARY: Exactly!

JOE: Look, love, we're in an airport, they've got a captive market, so the price goes up – it's supply and demand.

MARY: It's highway robbery, that's what it is!

JOE: Or airway robbery. Get it? Airway robbery!

MARY: Shut up, Joe. You're not funny, are you – never have been.

JOE: Fair point. I'll just keep quiet, dear.

MARY: And don't think I've forgotten about the sandwich.

JOE: Oh, will it ever end?

MARY: What was it again, brie and grape? I've never heard of the like, and (*sarcastically*) what a bargain at £4.39!

JOE: I was hungry!

MARY: I told you to fill up before we came out.

JOE: I've got an unstable metabolism.

MARY: No, love, you're just fat and greedy. Two coffees and a sandwich and it cost more than half our weekly shopping budget.

JOE: Anyway, what about you in the duty free?

MARY: What about it?

JOE: How much for that dribbly little bottle of perfume – thirty-odd quid!

MARY: I'll have you know that's a forty per cent saving on the high street price.

JOE: Oh, that's okay, then!

MARY: I don't know. If it was down to you I'd go around smelling like a skunk.

JOE: Oh, don't be daft. Not quite as bad as a skunk. . .

MARY: How much longer have we got to wait?

JOE: Boarding starts in about half an hour.

MARY: I hate waiting about. It's so boring. Let's check we've got everything.

JOE: We have done already, six times.

MARY: Well, you can't be too careful. Come on – passports?

JOE: Check.

MARY: Main luggage?

JOE: Checked in, receipt attached to boarding cards.

MARY: Hand luggage?

JOE: Safe and secure – yours, mine and the boy's.

MARY: Good, that's everything, then.

JOE: Yes, that's everything.

(*Pause: a moment of realisation that something is missing*)

MARY: Hang on a minute – where's your son?

JOE: What?

MARY: Don't 'what' me! Where's your son?

JOE: What's he done now? He's always 'my' son when he's done something wrong.

MARY: I don't know what he's done, 'cos I don't know where he is!

JOE: Eh? Well, he was with you. He went with you to the duty-free boutique to buy your trendy Britney Spears perfume.

MARY: No, I left him with you when you went to buy your ridiculously overpriced sandwich.

JOE: No, I was going to take him but you told me not to, otherwise he'd want a Coke and that would cost us another £1.79.

MARY: We've lost him! I don't believe it – we've lost our only son, you great dunderhead!

JOE: I'll find lost property and ask there.

MARY: He's not an umbrella!

JOE: Well, I'll go to information or something. You wait here.

(*JOE rushes off. MARY looks around frantically and then addresses the audience*)

MARY: Typical man. Can't trust them to do anything – not even the simplest task. I mean, my Joe, he's a carpenter by trade, but we've had a wobbly bookshelf in our lounge for I don't know how long, and will he fix it? Oh, I shouldn't complain. He's a good dad, good husband. He's taught the boy his trade – do anything for him. He's always been a difficult child – not behaviour-wise, he's as good as gold there, like a saint – but he's always been, well, let's say different. Like he's distracted or something. Shouldn't be surprised he's wandered off, really. Typical of him, absolutely typical.

JOE: (*Rushes on*) It's okay, love.

MARY: There you are! I've been worried sick.

JOE: Don't worry, he's fine.

MARY: Well, where is he? You haven't lost him again already?

JOE: No, we'll go and get him now, together. It's okay.

MARY: So where did you find him?

JOE: In the airport chapel.

MARY: The airport chapel! What's he doing there?

JOE: Just talking to people. He said to me, 'Where did you think I'd be, except for in my Father's house?'

MARY: Oh, that boy! Well, at least he's safe.

JOE: Exactly, safe and sound. Come on, let's go and get him.

MARY: Yeah, let's. I get the feeling this boy is going to cause me a lot of grief. A whole lot of grief. . .

BIBLE REFERENCE
Luke 2:41–52

It's a Party, innit!

'It's his loss, innit, not mine. Missing, like, the party of the year'

INTRODUCTION

You can have real fun with the very stylised and stereotypical characters in this piece. The party of the year becomes a little bit of a flop when Jane realises that all her mates have decided not to come along. Raquel is the bearer of the bad news, but is it quite so bad after all?

Characters: JANE; RAQUEL.

JANE is doing her hair and (heavily applied) make-up. RAQUEL enters, looking a bit sheepish.

JANE: Raquel, is that you?

RAQUEL: Yeah, just got back, haven't I.

JANE: Thank goodness for that. I'm having a right nightmare with my hair.

RAQUEL: What's wrong, then?

JANE: Well, it's all sticking up, innit.

RAQUEL: Come here, girl – blimey, what have you done?

JANE: My hair's never been the same since I started using that Laboratory Garnier stuff.

RAQUEL: What's wrong with it?

JANE: I dunno, do I. It just don't react well to my hair. Should've stuck with Head and Shoulders, innit.

RAQUEL: You look great! Make-up's good, too.

JANE: Yeah, I thought I'd go for the subtle look. Do you think I pulled it off?

RAQUEL: Oh yeah, very stylish.

JANE: Well, I gotta look the business tonight, haven't I, for my big party – ooh, I can't wait.

RAQUEL: Ah, I was going to talk to you about that.

JANE: (*Ignores*) And you know who's coming tonight – disco Dave! He's so fit, innit! Can't wait to, like, bust some grooves with him.

RAQUEL: He ain't coming.

JANE: (*Ignores*) And with me looking so hot, he won't be able to – (*Realisation*) What did you say, Raquel?

RAQUEL: He ain't coming, innit.

JANE: He ain't coming? Why?

RAQUEL: 'Cos he's just bought a field.

JANE: A field! What does he want a field for?

RAQUEL: I dunno, do I – probably for some raves or something, innit.

JANE: He's not coming to my party 'cos he's bought a field... I've heard some excuses in my time, innit, but that's just plain wrong.

RAQUEL: Tell me about it, sis. You must be well gutted.

JANE: I ain't even bothered, Raquel. To be honest, I always thought he was a bit of a minger anyway.

RAQUEL: That's the attitude, girl.

JANE: It's his loss, innit, not mine. Missing, like, the party of the year.

RAQUEL: He's not the only one though, is he?

JANE: What do you mean?

RAQUEL: Well, you know that hot guy called Hitch from down the club?

JANE: Oh yeah, the one who looks well like Orlando Bloom.

RAQUEL: Yeah, well, he ain't coming neither.

JANE: What's his excuse?

RAQUEL: He's just bought five yoke of oxen, innit.

JANE: Oxen? What's this city coming to?

RAQUEL: I know, but he says he's gotta try them out, so he can't come to the party.

JANE: This is bang out of order, Raquel! If word gets out that loads of people ain't coming, like, no one will come and I've bought loads of tortilla dips and bottles of WKD, innit.

RAQUEL: That's the problem, innit – the word on the street is that your party is not the cool place to be, and that anyone who comes will be, like, tarnished with a social stigma.

JANE: Coming to my party is a social stigma? That is well pathetic, innit. Still, at least there'll be us two.

RAQUEL: (*Pause*) That's what I wanted to talk to you about.

JANE: Oh no, you're kidding me.

RAQUEL: It's just I got this well nice new boyfriend, and he's asked me out tonight, innit.

JANE: So bring him along.

RAQUEL: Yeah, I would, but he's offered to cook me a well lush mushroom risotto.

JANE: Who is it?

RAQUEL: Disco Dave.

JANE: Disco Dave? I thought you said he was busy with his new field.

RAQUEL: Yeah, he is, sort of. He's setting up a little marquee for us and we is going to eat al fresco. It'll be well romantic.

JANE: So it's just me, then? Me and 240 bottles of WKD?

RAQUEL: I'm well sorry.

JANE: Whatever! I'll just have to throw my invitation net a bit wider.

RAQUEL: But everyone's turned you down, Jane.

JANE: Not just from our social circle – bunch of Judases! No,

I might invite some people from (*Inserts local place-name*). And if I can't get enough from there I may even invite the (*Inserts second local placename*) posse.

RAQUEL: Not (*Inserts second placename*)!

JANE: Why not? I is determined to have my party tonight, and if you won't come, someone else will. Now, if you don't mind, I gotta get busy with my invites.

RAQUEL: I'll see you later, then.

JANE: Yeah, whatever Trevor! Oh, and say hello to Disco Dave for me – the minger. (*RAQUEL leaves*) Now, where do I start? (*To the audience*) And what are youse all looking at? You checking me out or what? Do youse wanna come to my party tonight? I says, do youse wanna come to my party tonight? (*Fade to blackout as party music plays*)

BIBLE REFERENCE
Luke chapter 14

Contemporary

Panic

'But apart from the staff, missionaries, personnel and property so the work can grow, what do we need money for?'

INTRODUCTION

I've enjoyed performing this one a few times, and it works well at that embarrassing service where the church is having a pledge day or seeking to teach on the tricky topic of giving. Hopefully it raises a few giggles as well as making a thought-provoking point.

Characters: MAN; WOMAN.

MAN:	(*Astonished*) How much?
WOMAN:	You heard.
MAN:	How much?
WOMAN:	Now you're getting yourself into a tizzy.
MAN:	Well, are you surprised? Oh, you must be jesting.
WOMAN:	No, I'm not.
MAN:	I mean, that's quite some chunk of money you're talking about there, love! It's not just a few pennies.
WOMAN:	I know.
MAN:	It's going to mean some sacrifices.
WOMAN:	That is the general idea.
MAN:	Oh, I'm not talking to you.
WOMAN:	Oh dear, what a deep shame.
MAN:	(*Pause*) There's no emergency, is there? The church roof isn't caving in, is it?

WOMAN: No.

MAN: The church isn't subsiding – well, except in its theology, maybe.

WOMAN: No, darling, you're right. There's no alarming, life-threatening emergency.

MAN: So there you are. In which case, what do we need all this money for?

WOMAN: Well, for a start we've got to pay the staff, haven't we?

MAN: Have we?

WOMAN: Yes, of course we have.

MAN: Okay, but apart from the staff what do we need money for?

WOMAN: Missionaries. If you're in the back of beyond I suspect it's of some comfort to know that your sponsors are going to provide for you each month.

MAN: Okay, okay. But apart from the staff and the missionaries, what do we need money for?

WOMAN: More personnel and property, so the church can develop and grow in its mission. There's no end to the possibilities, really.

MAN: Oh, for goodness' sake! But apart from staff, missionaries, and personnel and property so the work can develop and grow, what do we need money for?

WOMAN: (*Pause*) I can't think of anything else specific at the moment.

MAN: Exactly! So if there's no emergency, what is all the blooming fuss about?

WOMAN: That's not how you're supposed to give, you prize prune! It's not about giving in a mad panic when there's some emergency. It's giving regularly, in a planned way, so the right hand is unaware of what the left hand is doing.

MAN: Oh, don't be so daft!

WOMAN: I'm not!

MAN: How can your left hand not know what your right hand is doing, dopey?

WOMAN: It's a metaphor, dear, meaning it's something you do quite naturally without making a big issue out of it.

MAN: I'm not making a big issue out of it, *actually*!

WOMAN: No, of course not, my mistake.

MAN: Anyway, what about Roger Measley?

WOMAN: What about him?

MAN: Well, he's absolutely loaded, isn't he, dripping in spondulix – and I bet he doesn't give half as much as you're suggesting.

WOMAN: How do you know?

MAN: Ah, well, I'll tell you. I was sitting next to him last Sunday and when the little velvet pouch came around I had a sneaky look – and guess how much he put in?

WOMAN: I don't know.

MAN: Guess!

WOMAN: A tenner.

MAN: No, try again.

WOMAN: I don't know, do I? Thirteen pence?

MAN: No! I'll tell you – nothing! Just flipped the bag towards me without a by-your-leave. Nothing!

WOMAN: So what? Very often I don't put anything in either.

MAN: What? Miss holier-than-thou casting all sorts of aspersions about me, and you don't put a red cent in yourself! That's a bit rum.

WOMAN: There are other, subtler ways of giving to the church without actually putting money in the bag. Not everyone's like you, wafting your arm around and showing off. . . (*She demonstrates*)

MAN: I do not!

WOMAN: No, dear, of course not, my mistake.

MAN: (*Pause*) So what shall we do tonight?

WOMAN: Oh, I don't mind, whatever.

MAN: Shall we get a DVD out?

WOMAN: Could do.

MAN: What sort of thing do you fancy?

WOMAN: For some reason I feel like something extremely violent.

MAN: I'll go and get one, then, shall I?

WOMAN: Okay.

MAN: Okay, then. Ooh, love, can you lend us a fiver? (*Lights fade to blackout as WOMAN digs in her bag*)

BIBLE REFERENCE
2 Corinthians 9:7

The Legend of Nottingham Forest

'Well, I still don't believe in any Jesus. I think it's all a load of rubbish'

INTRODUCTION

It is claimed that in our new, postmodern world people have rejected the concept of absolute truth. Truth is relative, and people can decide for themselves what is true or not. While this is a fair observation of society, I also find it interesting how we can so easily get fact confused with fiction. Take the multimillion-selling *Da Vinci Code*, or perhaps even the legend of Robin Hood. . .

Characters: MR BLOGGS; MRS BLOGGS; MASTER BLOGGS; MISS BLOGGS.

MR BLOGGS and MRS BLOGGS are seated centre stage. We hear loud music offstage.

MR:	Turn that racket down, Miss Bloggs! It's doing my head in! Sort her out, Mrs Bloggs, or I swear I'll go up and swing for her.
MRS:	Turn it down, Miss Bloggs! We can't hear ourselves think down here. Put your new headphones on or something! Oh, I give up.
MR:	That's it – I'm going to kill her. (*Music stops*) Ah, bliss!
MASTER:	(*Enters*) Hi ya.
MRS:	Hello, Master Bloggs.

MR: Oh, he's back at last. Where you been gadding off to, then?

MASTER: Just down the shops.

MR: Wiv your girlfriend!

MRS: Mr Bloggs!

MR: What? I'm only asking. Come on, then, Master Bloggs, which was it, birds or mates?

MASTER: It was a mixed group, if you must know.

MR: Woo-hoo! Mixed, eh? Anyone special we should know about?

MASTER: No!

MRS: Leave it be, Mr Bloggs.

MR: You can't even ask about your own family's well-being in this place. (*MISS BLOGGS enters, singing, with headphones on*) Oh, blimey!

MISS: Wanna listen, Mr Bloggs?

MR: I'd rather shove my ears in a blender.

MISS: Oh yeah, forgot you only like trendy rock 'n' roll.

MR: There's nothing wrong with rock 'n' roll – better than all that boom-boom-boom racket! Do us all a favour and switch it off a bit.

MISS: What's on the box tonight, then?

MRS: I'm just having a look.

MR: I wouldn't bother, Mrs Bloggs – bound to be a load of old tripe, as usual.

MISS: That don't stop you watching it twelve hours a day.

MR: Oh, very tactful, Miss Bloggs. You know it's a medical condition that confines me to my chair for most of the day.

MISS: Yeah, lazy-itus.

MRS: That's enough from you! Now, they've got that film *Robin Hood, Prince of Thieves* on at ten past eight.

MR: No, I hate him.

MISS: Who – Robin Hood?

MR: No! You can't hate Robin Hood – he's a national hero. I mean, I hate that Kevin Costner.

MRS: Ooh, I think he's gorgeous.

MR: You would. You fancy anything in a pair of trousers.

MASTER: How do you figure Robin Hood is a national hero, then?

MR: Well, he was, a few hundred years ago. It's a fact – robbing from the rich, giving to the poor, bit like an early Gordon Brown. You'd do well to watch it, Miss Bloggs, learn a bit of history.

MISS: I hate history.

MASTER: I'm sorry to disappoint you, but Robin Hood isn't actually an historical figure. He's just a legend, possibly loosely based on some facts.

MR: Don't be so daft, Master Bloggs, course he's real. If you'd gone up to Nottingham Forest all those years ago you'd have seen him yourself, cavorting around with his bows and arrows.

MISS: It's not Nottingham Forest, it's Sherwood Forest.

MR: Whatever! And there's his bit of stuff, Maid wotsername, and that big, fat, greedy monk.

MRS: Maid Marian and Friar Tuck.

MR: Exactly – case proved.

MASTER: Just because there's a Sherwood Forest, it doesn't automatically follow there's a Robin Hood.

MISS: What do you mean?

MASTER: Well, we've got a chimney, but it doesn't mean that Father Christmas comes down it, does it?

MRS: (*Upset*) Don't he?

MR: Shut up, Mrs Bloggs.

MISS: Anyway, you're a fine one to talk about myths and legends, Mr Christian! At least we don't believe in some airy-fairy Jesus.

MR: She's got a point, Master Bloggs.

MASTER: Well, not really. There's loads of evidence about the existence of Jesus.

MISS: If you believe the Bible.

MASTER: Not just in the Bible, in other historical works, too. In fact, there's probably more written about the existence of Jesus than figures such as Cleopatra or Caesar.

MR: Oh, so now you're saying Caesar didn't exist?

MASTER: No, I'm merely making the point that any historian would certainly accept the existence of Jesus, as they do Caesar's, but probably reject the accuracy of Robin Hood.

MRS: And what about Father Christmas?

MR: Oh, will you shut up about Father Christmas, Mrs Bloggs!

MISS: Well, I still don't believe in no Jesus. I think it's all a load of rubbish.

MASTER: That's your choice, Miss Bloggs, but I think you're in the minority. So, are we going to watch the film, then?

MR: I thought you said it was a load of rubbish.

MASTER: Well, it's still a good film.

MR: No, you've spoilt it now, saying it's a load of hocus pocus. What's on the other side, Mrs Bloggs?

MRS: Let's have a see. Ooh, *Gandhi*'s on in ten minutes.

MR: *Gandhi*? No, I don't fancy that.

MASTER: Why not?

MR: It's much too far-fetched.

(*MASTER buries head in disbelief, lights fade to blackout*)

Filthy Rags

'I've always believed in you, sort of. . . ish'

INTRODUCTION

This is certainly the sketch that I have performed the most over the years. As a monologue it is designed to pack rather a punch at the end, and on numerous occasions I have certainly got into some interesting conversations after performing it. Unlike some of the other pieces it really does need to be learnt rather than read.

Characters: PETER; VOICE (offstage only).

VOICE: (*Offstage*) Number 38 46 21 4, Mr Peter Benevolence, time to give your account, please. Thank you.

PETER rushes on, briefcase in hand. He looks directly to the front as he speaks to God.

PETER: Ah, hello. Do you mind if I just. . . ? (*He puts briefcase down and straightens jacket*) So, this is where I find out if I take the up or the down escalator, is it? Yes, well, I understand it's an account you want. It's very difficult to know where to start, really. But you know it's amazing how you always wonder about suffering some horrific death in a spectacular accident or from some life-draining disease. Well, I tell you, nothing, but nothing could have prepared me for my untimely demise. Picture the scene

– I'm walking to work, minding my own business, packed lunch of spam sandwiches safely stowed away in the briefcase, when all of a sudden, without any word of warning, *whack!* A great big chimney pot falls on top of my head! There was blood and gore and little bits of my skull scattered around all over the shop. It was a terrible mess, and the next thing I know, vroom, here I am! Unbelievable, isn't it? Totally unbelievable. *You* probably don't believe me. What am I talking about – of course you believe me, you probably planned it all. . . yes. . .

Anyway, back to my account. I had planned ahead in anticipation of a scenario such as this, so I've got everything possibly relevant recorded, logged and filed in my trusty briefcase. For starters, I've been a regular church-goer all my life. Every Christmas, every Easter, and a mass of weddings, funerals, christenings, etc etc. And on each occasion I've made a very generous donation to the church funds – of the rustling, not the rattling, kind, if you get my drift. Anyway, all this has been logged and receipted in the little black cash book which you'll find in the trusty briefcase. In addition to this I have records of my long and prolific history of regular and generous giving to charity. I'll name a few of the beneficiaries. There's been the RSPCA, RSPB, NCH, NSPCC, ABC, XYZ and the BFG – or is that a book? Anyway, all these records can also be found in the dark-green accounts book in the trusty briefcase. (*Ponders*) What else can I tell you about?

Oh, good deeds. Well, money doesn't solve everything, does it? And, to be honest, I've done it all, from charity jumble sales to helping old dears across the street. Everybody in my local area always knew, if there's anything you need any help with, you can always rely on trustworthy Peter Benevolence to give you a helping hand. Now, all this information, and more, can be found chronologically filed in the navy-blue file entitled 'Good Works', which you'll also find in the trusty briefcase.

Well, how am I doing? I think I've got everything covered. What more can I say? I've been a nice guy, good to my family and friends. On the religious side of things I suppose I've never been the fanatical type, but I don't necessarily see that as a bad thing, do you? Think of all the wars that have been kicked off in the name of religion – not to say that's your fault, of course! No, the point I'm trying to make is that my faith's always been much more of a personal thing really, just between me and – well, between me and me, I suppose! I've always believed in you, sort of. . . ish. Although I must admit it's quite overwhelming to actually meet you face to face like this. (*Short pause. Awaits response*) Well, say something, then! Aren't you going to say anything? No? It's not going too well, is it? What else can I say? If you don't believe me, all you need to do is look in the briefcase. Please? (*Loses temper*) Oh, why don't you just look in the briefcase, for God's – (*Stops himself*) I'm sorry! Look, please, just look in the briefcase.

(*PETER picks up the case. It falls open, spilling a pile of filthy rags and a letter that he reads*)

'All of us have become like one who is unclean, and all our righteous acts are like filthy rags. We all shrivel up like a leaf, and like the wind our sins sweep us away.' (*Pause*) Father, don't you remember me? (*Pause*) So, which escalator is it to be, then – up or – up or down? Thank you. Thank you.

(*PETER picks up briefcase, takes deep breath and exits*)

BIBLE REFERENCE
Matthew 7:21–23

The Round Triangle

'That, sir, is my personal affair. It has nothing to do with you!'

INTRODUCTION

Continuing our earlier theme of postmodernism and the shifting reality of truth, here's a short piece to introduce that topic in a humorous way. I mean, how far can we take this whole thing of 'truth is what you believe it to be'? Is it possible to argue that a circle is really a triangle?

Characters: ONE; TWO.

ONE: Good afternoon, sir.

TWO: Ah, good afternoon.

ONE: Is there anything I can help you with today, or are you just browsing?

TWO: I'm looking for a gift, actually.

ONE: Oh, how utterly charming! And who might the fortunate recipient be?

TWO: A work colleague. I'm looking for some small trinket as a token of our long friendship.

ONE: Oh, how *utterly* charming! Friendship is such a lost art form, I feel. In our postmodern world there's no time to think, let alone construct meaningful relationships.

TWO: You're probably right.

ONE: Still, no use whining, is there? We just need to get on with it and move with the times, don't we?

TWO: Indeed we do.

ONE: Anyway, listen to me going off on one – have you spotted anything you fancy?

TWO: I have, as a matter of fact. Can I take a closer look at that circular photo frame?

ONE: (*Affronted*) I beg your pardon?

TWO: The circular photo frame, just there – can I take a look?

ONE: I heard what you said first time, sir. I just couldn't believe my ears.

TWO: I'm sorry – I'm not sure what I've said to offend you.

ONE: Not sure what you've said? I find that hard to believe.

TWO: Look, I'm losing patience here. Just pass me that circular photo frame, will you?

ONE: There he goes again! How dare you?

TWO: How dare I what?

ONE: Boldly describe this photo frame as – circular.

TWO: Well it is, isn't it, a circle?

ONE: I've never been so offended in my life.

TWO: I can try a bit harder if you like.

ONE: Just because *you* believe this photo frame to be circular, sir, that doesn't give you the right to force your personal belief on anyone else, does it?

TWO: What are you talking about?

ONE: For instance, I could believe this was a square photo frame and find your calling it circular highly offensive.

TWO: And do you?

ONE: What?

TWO: Think it's square?

ONE: That, sir, is my personal affair! It's got nothing to do with you.

TWO: Oh dear, we're not getting very far here, are we?

ONE: That's because you're so obtuse! Really, the next thing you'll be saying is that my shirt is (*Insert the colour of the shirt that ONE is wearing*)

TWO: The thought had occurred to me.

ONE: I pity you. It seems to me that you are a very sad and narrow individual.

TWO: Well, what colour would you say it is?

ONE: People can believe whatever they like. I might decide to believe it's a kind of tawny brown.

TWO: Indeed you could, but of course you'd be totally wrong.

ONE: And there he goes again with his narrow, fundamentalist propaganda.

TWO: You really are a dimwit, aren't you?

ONE: I very well could be, sir. It's certainly your prerogative to believe what you choose.

TWO: (*Tries to calm things down*) Look, it seems we've got off on the wrong foot. I only came in here to buy a gift, not start a philosophical debate.

ONE: Of course, sir, you're absolutely right. I do apologise. I'm forever getting into these deep conversations.

TWO: Good. Well, let's start again, shall we?

ONE: Can I offer you a sweetie in recompense?

TWO: No, really, it's fine.

ONE: Oh, go on. I've got this box of Roses under the counter – everyone loves a Rose.

TWO: Oh, go on then.

ONE: Good. Now, which one would you like?

TWO: Erm, have you got any of those green triangles left?

ONE: Green triangles! How dare you?! I've never been so offended in my life! Get out, go on, buzz off! (*TWO exits as lights fade*)

Prayer Diary

'It's handy to know these things – just so I can put them in my prayer diary, you understand'

INTRODUCTION

I've used the characters of Joan and Mabel a number of times over the years, and if the truth be known I now feel very close to the pair of them! This sketch takes an amusing look, or perhaps swipe, at church prayer meetings. Valuable as the meetings obviously are, Joan and Mabel have rather missed the point, and the whole event becomes an information exchange – which is a polite way of saying 'gossip'! Of course, I'm not in the least suggesting this happens in my church, or indeed yours. Does it?

Characters: JOAN; MABEL.

JOAN and MABEL are seated onstage, sipping cups of coffee.

MABEL: Not a bad turn-out tonight, was it, Joany?

JOAN: Not bad at all, Mabel love, not bad at all.

MABEL: It's disgusting, though, really – I mean, where is people's commitment?

JOAN: I couldn't agree more, Mabel.

MABEL: Think about it, Joany. It's the midweek prayer meeting.

JOAN: I know.

MABEL: One hour, that's all it is – one measly hour.

JOAN: That's nothing in the grand scheme of things.

MABEL: But people can't tear themselves away from the telly, not for one hour.

JOAN: Understandable, though – *Coronation Street*'s hotting up
          a bit at the mo.

MABEL: You're not wrong there! Still, in this day and age
          people can video it.

JOAN: They just don't think, do they?

MABEL: No! My Henry said he'd tape it for me tonight – that's if
          the hopeless lummox can stay awake.

JOAN: My Charlie's the same, drops off every five minutes.

MABEL: Well, it's their age, isn't it? If you ask me, all they do
          past 65 is eat, sleep and go to the toilet. Sad, really – my
          Henry used to be so energetic.

JOAN: My Charlie, too. Here, talking about energetic, Father
          Humphrey looks a bit tired tonight, doesn't he?

MABEL: I thought that, very jaded. Look at the bags under his
          eyes.

JOAN: It's a real shame, isn't it?

MABEL: Listen, don't tell another soul this, Joany – it's strictly
          between you and me – but I was chatting to Jill who
          works at the doctor's surgery outside the Co-op this
          morning.

JOAN: Oh yes?

MABEL: Apparently, he's having terrible trouble with his diges-
          tive system at the moment. She absolutely swore me to
          secrecy, but I thought I'd tell you, just so you can put it
          in your prayer diary.

JOAN: Oh, I will.

MABEL: You know I don't gossip, that's not my style, but we do
          need to pray intelligently, don't we?

JOAN: Absolutely, Mabel.

MABEL: (*Pause*) Ooh, have you seen Mary Marshall over there?
          She makes you sick.

JOAN: Where?

MABEL: There! Flirting around Father Humphrey like a lovesick
          teenager.

JOAN: Oh, it's disgusting. She should know better at her age.

MABEL: Over him like a rash, she is. And look at the amount of make-up she's got caked on! Who does she think she is – Dolly Parton?

JOAN: It's mutton dressed as lamb, isn't it?

MABEL: She only comes to the prayer meetings for a flirt. I was watching her during the intercessions, just out of one eye, like.

JOAN: Oh, it's all wrong.

MABEL: She's directly in front of me on the telephone gossip chain. I mean prayer chain.

JOAN: Is she?

MABEL: Yeah, but I never know whether to believe a word she says.

JOAN: Oh, that's terrible.

MABEL: Tell me about it! You'll never guess what she called through the other week.

JOAN: Go on.

MABEL: Well, you know old William?

JOAN: William? Which one's that?

MABEL: You know! The one with the gammy foot that hands the hymn books out on a Sunday.

JOAN: Oh, William!

MABEL: Yes! Well, anyway, she phones me up, all in a dither, and tells me he's been rushed into hospital with gastroenteritis and an inflamed intestine.

JOAN: That sounds nasty.

MABEL: Ah, you wait! It turns out he had a mild case of trapped wind. How can you pray intelligently with her spinning yarns like that?

JOAN: Mind you, I wish my Charlie would get a dose of that.

MABEL: What, trapped wind?

JOAN: Yeah, he's got a severe case of the opposite, if you catch my drift!

MABEL: Oh, Joany, no! We're absolute martyrs, aren't we?

JOAN: (*Pause*) I notice that Jonathan, the nice youth leader, isn't here tonight.

MABEL: I noticed that, and Father Humphrey prayed a very odd prayer, didn't he?

JOAN: Very cryptic, I thought.

MABEL: Maybe I should have a quiet word with Father H., now Mary's prised herself away from him.

JOAN: I think that's an excellent idea, Mabel. It would come best from you.

MABEL: Nothing heavy, just a gentle dig for information.

JOAN: Well, you're known for your sensitivity.

MABEL: It's just good to know what's going on, just so I can put them in my prayer diary.

JOAN: Precisely.

MABEL: I find it so much more effective if I can pray intelligently.

JOAN: My sentiments exactly.

MABEL: Right, you go and get us a coffee refill, and I'll have a quiet word. Rendezvous back here in five.

JOAN: Okay, good luck! (*JOAN exits*)

MABEL: (*Pause. She straightens her blouse*) Father Humphrey? Ah, just a quiet word with you, if I may? (*MABEL exits as if toward Father Humphrey as lights fade*)

BIBLE REFERENCE
Proverbs 26:22

Introducing Bob

'Don't be defeatist, don't be shy, but don't be too over the top'

INTRODUCTION

This sketch and slight variations on the theme have come out at church when we are promoting a new evangelistic course. We tried to tackle the issues of the fear of inviting people, and people's perceived reluctance to sign up for a course lasting a number of weeks. The course we were promoting at the time was called 'Introducing God', and the taster event was called 'The Couch' – these references can easily be doctored to suit your needs with a bit of thought – over a twenty-minute cup of coffee. The sketch starts with ONE doing a standard advert for a course that TWO interrupts from the congregation.

Characters: ONE; TWO; THREE; GROUP (to hold up sign advertising 'The Couch' event).

ONE is onstage delivering a sign-up advert for the church's new evangelistic course. TWO interrupts from the congregation before going onstage.

TWO: It's all very well you babbling on about this course, but it's not that easy to get people to come along, is it?

ONE: What do you mean?

TWO: (*Joins ONE onstage*) Well, how can you subtly slip into conversation, 'Hi, would you like to come on a seven-week course?'

ONE: Well, obviously you don't do it quite like that.

TWO: What do you suggest then, clever clogs?

ONE: I can suggest a few pitfalls to avoid, if that would help.

TWO: Try me.

ONE: Well, firstly, don't be defeatist. Be positive about asking someone – unlike candidate number one. . .

TWO: Ah, hello, Roger!

ONE: Hello, Paul.

TWO: Look, now, I was just wondering if you might come to this thing. I'm sure you probably wouldn't, but in case you did, I thought I'd ask you anyway. Of course you won't – far too busy, and you find me an irritating, wussie Christian, but it's okay if you don't – it's there, it's free, you're very welcome, but I won't be offended by rejection, I'm used to rejection. So, would you like to?

ONE: Can you tell me any more?

TWO: No, I thought not – well, no offence taken. Ta-ra!

ONE: So, be positive and listen.

TWO: Okay, what else?

ONE: Be bold. Don't be afraid to share with people what the course is about and why it's important – unlike candidate number two. . .

TWO: Ah, hello, Roger!

ONE: Hello, Paul.

TWO: I was wondering if you'd be interested in coming to a course I'm helping with?

ONE: Oh yes, at your church, is it?

TWO: No, not at the church! It's at the arts centre, actually.

ONE: Oh, very swish – what's it called?

TWO: Called? Oh yes, it's called Introducing G– (*Hesitates*) Introducing G– (*Hesitates*) Introducing Bob.

ONE: Introducing Bob?

TWO: Yes, Introducing – (*Clears throat*) Bob.

ONE: Well, what's it about?

TWO: Oh, everything – life, the universe, love, death, sacrifice. . . poodles, and, erm, G–, G–, Bob.

ONE: Bob?

TWO: Yes, Bob.

ONE: So, be bold. You might be surprised at the positive response you get.

TWO: Any more pitfalls?

ONE: One more.

TWO: Go on, then.

ONE: Well, don't be defeatist, don't be shy, but don't be over the top.

TWO: Over the top?

ONE: Yes.

TWO: Like what?

ONE: Like candidate number three. . .

TWO: Ah, Roger!

ONE: Paul!

TWO: Can I ask you a question?

ONE: Fire away.

TWO: Are ye drenched in the sacrificial blood of the lamb?

ONE: I beg your pardon?

TWO: Are ye covered in the blood of the lamb?

ONE: No, don't think so – I'm a veggie.

TWO: Well, you need to be saved, brother. You need to be justified, holified, sanctified and rectified.

ONE: You think so?

TWO: I know so! And I would like to introduce you to God. To Elohim. To Jehovah. To (*Spells the letters*) YHWH.

ONE: YHWH?

TWO: Yes, that's 'Yahweh' without the vowels.

ONE: Let me have a think – maybe.

TWO: Not for too long, brother – the clock is ticking!

ONE: So, be positive and bold, but natural and not totally OTT.

TWO: One more snag.

ONE: What's that?

TWO: Seven weeks is a long time. People may not be keen to sign up. Is there any way they can get a taster?

ONE: Funny you should say that – yes, there is.

(*GROUP walks toward stage carrying sign advertising taster event – in this case called 'The Couch'*)

TWO: Hold on – what are you doing?

THREE: Us?

TWO: Yes, you!

THREE: Advertising 'The Couch' event.

TWO: No, wrong week – we're advertising 'Introducing God' this week.

THREE: Yeah, us too.

TWO: What – you're introducing God to the couch?

THREE: No! 'The Couch' next Sunday is an introduction to 'Introducing God'.

TWO: You're introducing 'Introducing God'?

THREE: Yep – well, actually we're introducing introducing 'Introducing God'.

TWO: Now I'm totally confused.

ONE: That's what I was about to say. If you've got a friend who might be interested, bring them to 'The Couch' event, and it might whet their appetite to find out more. Then you can invite them on the course.

TWO: Well, why didn't you say? That all sounds perfectly logical. . .

Two Seekers

'Even if some bloke really did what he did, it still doesn't change anything'

INTRODUCTION

This piece is a duologue in which the two performers don't respond to one another but direct thoughts to the audience. The idea is for use at an evangelistic event, to try to challenge people to have an open mind and make the journey from being sceptics to asking some serious questions. In a sense it is a companion piece to 'Introducing Bob' and would go down well at a taster event for some kind of Alpha or evangelistic course. The sketch is in three short acts. They can be performed at different points in the service or together, with some short incidental music and lighting change to indicate change of act.

Characters: MAN; WOMAN.

The MAN and WOMAN are both seated onstage. They take it in turns to address the audience.

ACT ONE

MAN: God? I mean, do I look like I care?

        Yeah, I guess he might exist, but what I can say for certain is that whether he does or not has absolutely no effect on me and my life whatsoever. I'm not one to boast, but come on, I've done pretty well for myself, haven't I? And I'm happy. Not bad-looking, half-decent football player, nice job, nice car, nice pad, plenty of quality mates – what more could you ask for? Well, that Keira Knightley wouldn't go amiss, for starters! But seriously, why on earth would I need some airy-fairy bloke up in the clouds?

No, you can have him. I'll stick to following my gods, like Arsenal and my real, human friends.

WOMAN: Oh, don't get me started on that one – hasn't anyone told you? You're better off not talking about religion to me. I get really annoyed with it, all of it! Anyone running around trying to tell me to change, to have some ridiculous belief in a load of old tosh can forget it. Come on, pull the other one! I mean, it is so obvious – there is no God. But some people who just can't hack it in the real world need something to give them a bit of comfort. When the going gets tough, they say a little prayer to the Lord and hope all will be okay. Do me a favour! It'd be much better if we just gave up on this make-believe story and got on with living!

ACT TWO

MAN: I met her at the polo club – posh venue, posh totty, pleasantries exchanged, drinks purchased, wading in at my most charming. All going according to plan until one nugget of info trips me right up. She's a flipping Christian! Would you credit it? And not a pretend one, like Britney Spears – she even goes to church! Yeah! And she's normal, not weird or anything, and she was enjoying herself! A Christian, enjoying herself! Whatever next?

Well, undeterred and out to impress, I showed my religious sensitivity by suggesting going to see that Mel Gibson Jesus film. She says, 'Ooh, yeah!' I say, 'Get in!' Now, as far as date movies go, I think a romcom would have been more advisable – the Gibson film's not exactly a feel-good giggle-fest, is it? Anyway, she was really moved. (*Pause*) So was I. Can't stop thinking about it, if I'm honest. I mean, what if some bloke really did – y'know – what he did?

WOMAN: Everyone said she'd had a good innings, and she did, I suppose. Still, doesn't stop me being upset, grandma not being here any more. Can't help thinking where she is. Just disappeared? She can't have. At the funeral some quaint old friend of hers said something about her being in a 'better place'. Well, it's not that hard if you look around here, is it? I must admit, though, it's a nice thought, and, well, I really want grandma to be happy. But it's just a fairy tale, isn't it? Designed to make us feel better, right?

Funnily enough, she thought it was a lot more than that. In the last few years she never bothered speaking to me about what she believed – gave up, I suppose. But back when I was a kid, before I knew better, she would tell me Bible stories – tell me about Moses and David, about Mary and about Jesus, who loved me even more than she did. I thought I'd forgotten all about that. Until now.

MAN: Even if some bloke really did what he did, it still doesn't change anything.

WOMAN: Oh, pull yourself together, woman! Fond reminisces of childhood and some old story don't change anything!

BOTH: Do they?

ACT THREE

MAN: Here I am! What? Don't laugh!

It's not because of her that I'm in church. It's not! Well, maybe just a little bit. My mates were giving me right grief when they heard I was off to church, 'Bless me, Father, for I have sinned' and all that. But I want to find out more, really – so sue me!

And that film. I just can't get it out of my head. Some of those images of what he did, for all those people, how he forgave them. Anyway, I had to see what it was all about. Don't get me wrong – I'm not signed up or anything. It's not like I've suddenly seen the light!

WOMAN: So I kept on thinking about this God stuff after the funeral and decided to do a bit of casual research. Googled it on the Internet, even asked Jeeves, but a fat lot of good he was.

Then it hit me. When I popped into the village the other day to get my nails done, I couldn't find a car parking space to save my life – you know what it's like. Well, between you and me, I have a confession to make. I parked it in the church's private car park. I did feel a bit cheeky, but I thought, well, Christians are the forgiving sort. When I got back, there was a flyer on the windscreen about some seeker event, so I thought, why not come along? That's it, mind! Don't get any funny ideas. I just came in to have a little look.

MAN: 'Cos there's no harm asking questions, is there?

WOMAN: I just want to find out a little bit more.

BOTH: You'd be daft not to. (*Lights fade*)

The Secret

'I'm sorry, it's just that it was such a good thing I couldn't keep it a secret'

INTRODUCTION

That's the problem with secrets. Some of them are just so good, so exciting, that you just can't keep them a secret. This short piece illustrates how we are at gossiping the gospel: is it something we are so excited about we like to share it, or is it our best-kept secret?

Characters: DAD; GIRL; MUM.

GIRL is excitedly singing and decorating a gift. DAD enters.

DAD: Hello, darling.

GIRL: Hello, daddy.

DAD: How are you getting on with that?

GIRL: Fine, thank you, daddy.

DAD: Is it ready for mummy yet?

GIRL: Nearly – I just want to decorate it with a pretty pink bow.

DAD: Oh, what a lovely idea! I'm sure mummy will love that.

GIRL: Yes, she will, 'cos she told me that pink is her most favourite colour in the whole wide world.

DAD: Well, all girls love pink, don't they, darling?

GIRL: I don't.

DAD: Whyever not, darling?

GIRL: It used to be my most favourite colour in the whole wide world until a girl in my school called Stacy Wilson – eucchh! – started wearing pink the whole time.

DAD: What difference does that make?

GIRL: She's bossy and smelly and nearly every day she wees herself.

DAD: That's not very nice, darling.

GIRL: No, it isn't, especially if you're sitting next to her.

DAD: Enough of that, now! Poor little Stacy. And it most certainly shouldn't stop a pretty young girl liking the colour pink.

GIRL: Daddy! It is a rash and sexist generalisation to suggest that all girls like pink and proves that you are inappropriately affected by our male-dominated society.

DAD: Have you been listening to mummy?

GIRL: Yes.

DAD: Well, shut up and stick the bow on the present.

GIRL: (*Arranges bow*) When is mummy home?

DAD: Very soon, so we must hide the present.

GIRL: Okay.

DAD: And darling –

GIRL: Yes, daddy?

DAD: This is mummy's very special birthday present, isn't it?

GIRL: Yes, daddy.

DAD: And when is mummy's birthday?

GIRL: Thursday 7 October 2007.

DAD: Good girl. And what does that mean?

GIRL: (*Pause*) She'll be very old.

DAD: No – well, I must admit she's no spring chicken any more.

GIRL: What does that mean?

DAD: It doesn't matter. What does matter is what I said in the car on the way home from the shops. (*GIRL giggles*) What are you laughing at?

GIRL: You said a word that my teacher said is very rude and you said it to the other driver and stuck some of your fingers out of the window.

DAD: Yes, well, forget about that. What else did I say about mummy's present?

GIRL: Oh! That it was a very special surprise birthday present for mummy and it was a secret between you and me.

DAD: Exactly.

GIRL: I'm a clever girl, aren't I, daddy?

DAD: You are very clever indeed.

MUM: (*Offstage*) Hello, I'm home!

DAD: Hello love! Now, remember our little secret. (*DAD and GIRL both sshh as if in a conspiracy as MUM enters*)

MUM: Hello – what are you both playing at?

GIRL: We both have got a secret, and it's that we've bought you a surprise birthday present of a jewellery box, and I've wrapped it in paper and a pretty pink bow and hidden it in the drawer. (*GIRL smiles*)

DAD: Unbelievable!

GIRL: (*Realises*) Oh sorry! Sorry, daddy!

MUM: Don't worry, darling. I still won't open it until my birthday.

DAD: Oh, whatever. Really, sweetheart, why did you have to tell mummy? I thought it was our special secret.

GIRL: I'm sorry. It's just that it was such a good thing I couldn't keep it a secret.

MUM: Yes, darling, come on – some things are too good to keep secret, don't you agree?

DAD: Maybe. Anyway, what's for dinner? I'm starving.

GIRL: Told you – male-dominated society.

MUM: What was that, darling?

DAD: Ignore her – she's trying to be clever.

GIRL: I am clever! You told me I was.

DAD: That was when I thought you could keep a secret!

GIRL: Whatever! Can I ask you another question, mummy?

MUM: Of course you can, darling.

GIRL: Daddy just said that you weren't a spring chicken any more. What does that mean?

DAD: Oh no!

MUM: What does it mean? Well, for a start it means daddy will be cooking the tea tonight! (*DAD sighs and exits as lights fade*)

BIBLE REFERENCE
Matthew 28:11–20

Calling on the Lord

'There's no need to swear – I was only asking!'

INTRODUCTION

It always blows my mind to think that God is everywhere, all the time. I guess it's something that our finite minds will never quite grasp. But just imagine if every time his name was called he made a personal appearance in order to see what the problem was – even if his name was called in less than positive circumstances! Now, that would give you the shock of your life!

Characters: ROGER; GOD.

ROGER is sitting at a table reading a newspaper. GOD stands in the back-ground. ROGER spills his coffee.

ROGER: Oh, God Almighty! (*GOD slowly walks across and joins ROGER at the table*)

GOD: Hello.

ROGER: Oh, hello. These stupid coffee lids – they should redesign them, don't you think?

GOD: Oh well, I've never had a problem with them, to be honest.

ROGER: Then you're a better man than me.

GOD: Nice of you to say so. Was there something you needed help with?

ROGER: Er, help? No.

GOD: Oh, only I thought I heard you call out.

ROGER: What? Oh well, yes – it was just a general expletive, you know. I spilt my skinny latte all down my trousers.

GOD: Oh, I see! You'd probably have been better off calling out for Mr Muscle then, or the Cillit Bang man.

ROGER: What are you on about?

GOD: Well, they do a great job with stains, so I've heard.

ROGER: Thanks, I'll bear that in mind.

GOD: That's why I'm here – to help.

ROGER: Sorry, who are you?

GOD: Well, you should know.

ROGER: I beg your pardon.

GOD: God Almighty.

ROGER: There's no need to swear – I was only asking!

GOD: No, you don't understand. I am God Almighty.

ROGER: (*Pause*) As in *the* God Almighty?

GOD: Yep.

ROGER: The all-powerful creator of the world?

GOD: There's only one of me, as far as I'm aware, and I'm omniscient, so I'm aware of everything!

ROGER: And you're here in Starbucks?

GOD: Yes, you called out for me, remember?

ROGER: Oh, I see where you're going here.

GOD: But as it turned out you didn't need the creator of the universe, just the creator of a reliable cleaning product.

ROGER: Yes, well, I'm sorry about that. I know it's out of order calling out your name like that. Must be quite annoying.

GOD: Not at all. I love it when people call on my name. Just do me a favour – think about me when you do it, and why you're doing it.

ROGER: Yeah, of course.

GOD: I've known you since before you were born. I knew you before you were formed in your mother's womb. I know everything about you.

ROGER: (*Pause*) When you say 'everything'. . .

GOD: I mean everything. There have been plenty of times you could have called on me – I wish you had, but you didn't. It breaks my heart, but I won't force myself.

ROGER: I'm sorry.

GOD: Why do people use my name to curse?

ROGER: I don't know. Because. . . I don't know. I'm sorry.

GOD: You're forgiven. (*GOD exits. ROGER sits in silence for a moment. He wipes his trousers and exits as lights fade*)

BIBLE REFERENCE
Psalm 139

In the Dark

'Well, for crying out loud, why didn't you turn it on?'

INTRODUCTION

Let's finish off with a fun one that can be used in a wide variety of settings. Its main thrust is to illustrate how daft it is to have at our fingertips the transforming word of God through the pages of Scripture when so often we don't bother to delve in. It's about as silly as being in a blackout with a torch in your pocket and not turning it on!

Characters: DAVE; NICK.

The stage is in blackout.

DAVE: Oh, this is the third time this week!

NICK: Typical, innit?

DAVE: It's just not good enough.

NICK: Not much we can do about it, is there?

DAVE: Oh, stop being so philosophical. What with the money you pay, you expect a better service.

NICK: At least it saves on the bill.

DAVE: Eh?

NICK: Well, if it's cut off, the meter won't be running, so the bill will be less.

DAVE: What an odd way of looking at it.

NICK: I know, but it's true.

DAVE: It's the inconvenience of it, though. It stops you doing what you need to be doing.

NICK: Like what?

DAVE: Well, whatever!

NICK: You weren't doing anything. You never are. You're so boring.

DAVE: That's not the point! The point is. . . Well, the point is obvious.

NICK: (*Pause*) Wanna play a game?

DAVE: Like what?

NICK: I spy. Get it – I spy!

DAVE: Oh, very funny! Now, where's the sofa? (*DAVE stubs toe*) Agh!

NICK: What is it?

DAVE: I've just stubbed my toe.

NICK: Ooh, I bet that hurts.

DAVE: Yes, it does! Who put that there?

NICK: What?

DAVE: That!

NICK: What is it?

DAVE: Well, I don't know, we're in pitch black!

(*Lights suddenly go on*)

DAVE: Oh, hallelujah!

NICK: See, it never takes long. A few tweaks and it's all back to normal.

DAVE: Speak for yourself. My toe is still throbbing.

NICK: Oh, stop moaning. I'll go and put the kettle on.

DAVE: Wait a minute.

NICK: What?

DAVE: What's that in your hand?

NICK: What, this old thing?

DAVE: Yes, that old thing.

NICK: I dunno.

DAVE: You don't? It's a torch, isn't it?

NICK: Might be.

DAVE: Have the batteries run out?

NICK: Don't think so.

DAVE: Well, test it out, then.

NICK: (*He tests*) Nope, looks perfectly okay.

DAVE: Wonderful! And how long have you been holding on to that perfectly functioning torch?

NICK: Can't remember.

DAVE: Did you have it during the blackout?

NICK: Er. . .

DAVE: You did, didn't you?

NICK: Yeah, I did.

DAVE: So, let me get this straight. During the blackout, while we were stumbling around in the dark, while I was causing myself permanent physical damage, you were clutching hold of a working torch.

NICK: I suppose that's a fair summary.

DAVE: Well, for crying out loud why didn't you turn it on?

NICK: I couldn't be bothered.

DAVE: Couldn't be bothered! Well, it's not exactly a great hardship.

NICK: I thought we were coping quite well without it.

DAVE: And you didn't think a little bit of light to guide our paths might be in any way helpful?

NICK: Well, now you put it like that.

DAVE: (*Pause*) Couldn't be bothered! Put the kettle on. Do something useful for once.

(*Blackout*)

DAVE: Oh, not again!

NICK: That's the fourth time this week now.

DAVE: Any bright ideas?

NICK: Erm. . . Ooh, how about a game? I've got it – I spy with my little eye –

DAVE: Oh, get me out of here!

(*Incidental music to close piece*)

BIBLE REFERENCE
2 Timothy 3:16–17

Index of Bible passages

50 Sketches About Jesus

by David Burt

Picture the scene: Jesus preaching at Wembley Stadium; a paparazzi photographer in Bethlehem; Mary cooking spaghetti hoops on toast; the wise men shopping in Harrods.

Strange? Maybe. Funny? Certainly. But every sketch here highlights a truth about Jesus of Nazareth that is relevant to life today.

There's something here for all levels of expertise, and all ages. Fully indexed by themes, occasions and Bible references, this is an ideal resource for churches and other groups who wish to communicate old truths in fresh ways.

'A bumper bran-tub of breezy curtain-raisers on a host of topics which may particularly appeal to church drama groups with small casts and limited resources.'

Paul Burbridge, Riding Lights Theatre company

 **Kingsway**

www.kingsway.co.uk